THE BLACK MAN'S ANSWER

(A Common Man's Perspective on the Black Struggle)

Written By

J. G. Robinson

Balante Publishing LLC
Publisher

BALANTE PUBLISHING

Balante Publishing LLC
Publisher
2226 Bowlin CT
Chesterfield, VA 23235
(804) 426-1797

ISBN-13: 978-0-9995150-1-3
ISBN-10: 0999515012

<u>Acknowledgements</u>

I would like to give a special thanks to my mother Betty Jones who was the foundation for all I knew, believed, and experienced while growing up as a young boy in this world. I would also like to give my appreciation to Greg Jones as the man who helped raise me and the only man whom I shall ever call my father.

My undying gratitude goes out to my wife Aquoyah Robinson, who endured countless conversations with me regarding the topics found within this book. As well as my children Perrisha, Draven, Tezdon, and Acacia, who unbeknownst to them provided an endless source of inspiration and motivation for me to pull from.

Furthermore, I would like to personally thank my last remaining childhood friend Rodney E. Hill. Who regardless of our many disagreements served as a reliable sounding board for many years regarding the ideals spoken about in this book. I would also like to thank my entire extended family who are too numerous to name individually, but hail primarily out of Belle Glade, Florida. It was the deep seeded desire to cure our ills as a family and bring us all together that sparked the original urge to create this book.

Next, I would like to thank my trusted friend Deborah Turner Muhammad. She was the first person I met to believe in my ability to be more than the average person. I also have to acknowledge the United States Military for being the main platform in which I was able to gain so many unique and different experiences to draw from that helped me grow as an individual.

Lastly to the person whom I loved, cherished, and miss the most. My great grandmother Mattie M. Campbell. She was just a young farm girl from Elba, Alabama who undoubtedly affected my entire existence before departing this world. I humbly dedicate this book in her honor.

Contents

Public Address

To all who will read this, I greet you. I greet you in the same revolutionary spirit as Toussaint L'Ouverture as he heroically fought for independence against the French. With the insightful vision of Booker T. Washington as he strategically helped lay the foundation for the Tuskegee Institute and as the catalyst of change W.E.B Du Bois craved while assisting in the establishment of the NAACP. I reach out to you all consciously promoting the innovative genius of those such as Madam C. J. Walker who crushed the economic barriers around her to become the first black millionaire in America, and to awaken others existing today, whose potential still has yet to be revealed.

Please take note as the ideals illustrated in this piece carry the same racial pride and confidence that rang out in the voice of Marcus Garvey as he spoke to the masses in places like Harlem, New York. While simultaneously striving for peace, harmony, and unity amongst us all as the Reverend Martin Luther King Jr. did marching down the streets of the old segregated south here in America.

It is from these remarkable lives and resilient spirits, along with many others not mentioned, that I've derived the inspiration and motivation required to produce the concepts conceived in the pages to follow. My current formal education level is neither that of a Doctor, Scholar, Professor, Lawyer, Preacher, Politician, Therapist, Dietician, Economist, Scientists, Anthropologist, Historian, Psychologist, nor Ivy League graduate of any kind. I boast only my life experience in this world as a proud descendant of my enslaved African ancestors.

Therefore, I present this humble attempt to explain the enigma known as racism and inequality that presently plagues my fellow black Americans with the hope it will provide some guidance to those in other cultures as well.

This book is meant to positively guide, answer, reinforce, and influence the lifestyles of those in the black community. Many of which may need a little assistance finding stability, dealing with issues, or simply making progress within their lives. It should serve as quick reference tool to the common man of any race or culture, to understanding the factors that produce the everyday realities observed within the African American culture.

Furthermore, the message within is meant to be read objectively as there is no one way to view, interpret, perceive or remedy every ailment concerning our people. This book should be used as a moral measuring stick of sorts in which to calculate our current state of being. As well as a tool to help identify potential room for growth and improvement within our lives and culture.

In any case, it should at a minimum provide a good starting point for us even if only to bring about a higher state of consciousness, awareness, and understanding concerning these issues amongst us all.

Preface

Knowledge of self

We as the black community need to understand one major concept which is that nothing can be as effective at holding a people back as the flaws held within themselves. Therefore, the first issues needing to be addressed are how to eliminate or at least reduce the amount of ignorance, apathy, and other undesirable traits that some have come to develop within our culture thus far.

Culture

Over time the combined results of multiple individuals establishing a similar way of life becomes known as that people's culture. Some African Americans may suffer from a serious lack of culture due to poor education and poverty that stems directly from our ancestors being oppressed during slavery.

This in turn causes many of us who grew up in these conditions to accept the way we were raised (which may seem inappropriate to others) as the way "black life" should be for all of us and therefore make no attempt to change it for the next generation.

We must first admit this is occurring so appropriate steps can be taken to assist those who need it. Doing so should grant us better control of the perceptions we put out into society about ourselves. We should also monitor what behaviors we allow from outside the culture to influence us in our homes and communities.

Respect

Respect is a necessity for us individually and collectively as a whole. A black man needs to feel respected by his fellow brethren as well as his black woman, friends, and family members. The same can be said for many black women who deserve to have their proper place on the throne beside us as the respected queens we know they have been in our lives. It's time we get back to the basics and transition this from a dream to a reality amongst our people.

Economics

The basics of managing money are a must! Not only how to earn it, but how to invest it back into ourselves. This is needed in order to break the cycle of poverty and leave an inheritance behind for our youth instead of bills and debts that need to be paid. This is probably one of the most important things not properly taught to us in our public school systems. Truth be told, most problems in our communities can be broken down into a simple matter of economics more so than racism. However, we have to teach each other how to identify and distinguish between the two. It's time we learn the difference and stop playing into the social rhetoric and political propaganda.

Perceptions

Sadly, I have witnessed many examples in which we as blacks have displayed distrust for other blacks. Not that we don't have our reasons for doing so, but it's an issue that should be addressed as it is a significant factor in our inability to unite. The message needs to sink in that we must love, tolerate, and depend on each other in order to live happily together. There is no reason why a young black male can't go into an unknown hood or housing project he's never been to and not be embraced with a genuine smile and warm conversation by those who already live there. It's time we really breakdown why certain areas have this problem and figure out how to begin repairing the psychological damage already done. We can achieve this while simultaneously rebuilding the trust that should be prevalent in our communities.

Civic Responsibility

Far too often are scenes of broken glass, aluminum cans, plastic bags, used condoms, cigarette butts, and the occasional faint smell of urine, a common backdrop in our environments. This I feel is attributed to a lack of ownership in our community. For most the rule is simple; "if it's not ours, then who cares?"

While others may simply move if it gets too bad around the area, neither of which would be appealing options if the property we lived in was actually owned by us. Steps need to be taken to ensure we spend less time being tenants and more time being the owners of property in our own communities. This would greatly improve the sense of responsibility among most.

In the meantime, we should stress the value of volunteering and completing productive projects to ensure a certain level of pride is maintained our towns. Doing so will help us feel better about the things we currently have that's worthwhile in the community and give the upcoming generations something to strive for in the future. It's important for us to understand how living in areas that are often vandalized, trashy, or unsafe, can warrant a lack of respect from those in and outside of our community.

Communication

Good communication cannot be emphasized enough. Every aspect in a person's life can and will be influenced by their ability to communicate effectively with those around them. It is an absolute must for all, as it is the primary way to solve the future problems we will encounter over and over again in our lives.

Civic Respect

We must ensure that we know our rights and utilize them when it's time to vote and when dealing with the police and other civil authorities. For instance, if the door of a nearby home gets kicked in unlawfully by the police, we should not only be "aware" our rights have been violated but know how to properly address the issue. This way we can stick up for ourselves and our neighbors across the street if they should find themselves in the same position. This should reduce the chances of us being taken advantage of by expensive lawyers and improper police procedures.

Overall Awareness

As African Americans we must stress the importance of maintaining our right to vote and the power that can be wielded by exercising a strong political voice. It should become routine for us to approach the county school board if needed when issues arise with our children's education. We can collectively petition City Council or call our Congressman as well when decisions are being made that will affect our communities.

No one should be able to re-zone our districts and put up a strip club or liquor store near our kid's schools, parks, or local churches without our community being aware, and if needed take actions against it. Now I'm not saying everyone's got to run for President of the United States of course, but we should at least know how to go about getting a simple "stop sign" placed at the end of our streets if needed.

Patriotism

Often a very controversial subject, it seems many of us are confused on how to take our nationality. I personally feel all of us here are American with an obvious lineage to our African ancestry. Therefore, I confidently feel we have every reason to claim, "**ALL RIGHTS AFFORDED TO AN AMERICAN!**" Let's face it, we've shed our blood from the cotton fields to the battlefields for this nation and we need to affirm that in our culture. Furthermore, I feel the only thing more ignorant than those who say blacks aren't Americans, are the uneducated people who believe it.

Health

It's important we monitor our health as much as possible. Physical, mental, emotional, and spiritual well being all need to be maintained and balanced in order for a person to achieve peace and happiness in this world. This directly affects a person's self esteem, confidence, and inherently the overall ability for us to believe in ourselves.

Discipline

The most fundamental tool for achieving any level of success in life is discipline. It's not enough to just sit around talking, hoping, wishing, and praying for progress and change, we must take action. We must reinforce the level of discipline in our lives and those around us to make sure we stay on track with our goals.

For some of us the concept of setting goals in itself needs to be established. If properly practiced over time we should become more skilled at setting and achieving the goals we all desire. With enough practice we can also assist those we love and care about with meeting their goals as well.

<u>Selflessness</u>

It goes without saying that many of us who reside in low income communities require a daunting amount of work to achieve unity and peace amongst ourselves. I will be the first to say we need to achieve reasonable progress in this category before trying to do anything for others outside of our race.

Nevertheless, we do have to acknowledge the fact that we aren't the only people in the world to have struggled or suffer a history of hardship. It is imperative we demonstrate to other cultures that we are open, receptive, and willing to participate in their causes as well.

Whether it be to the Latino, the Arab, the Asian, the Native American, the Jew, the Muslim, and **"YES"** even the white man. We must show we are a positive force not only for ourselves but others as well. This will serve as the invisible finish line in our struggle for progress. The world is bigger than the African American community and being able to collectively admit that is a huge sign we've grown as a people.

Chapter 1
Knowledge of Self

COPING WITH FEAR

Growing up as a young child in Central Florida, I noticed certain disparities between the way my fellow African American people lived, as opposed to other cultures. As time passed and I grew older, I began to dissect these differences and ponder the circumstances that caused them. Many of these differences could be seen in the way we spoke, the ideas we had, and the actions we took or lack thereof when it came to everyday decision making.

Most people called me weird for thinking about such things so much. Others I knew would tell me to stop "over thinking" life altogether. Nonetheless, my inquisitive mind would not allow me to stop asking questions about how these things came to be for our people. Each answer I received only caused further analysis of our culture here in America. It also created a burning desire for me to solve the issues that plagued our community. As I dug deeper I realized that one common root to many of our issues is a little human trait known as fear.

According to data published by *The State of Working America*, "blacks held the highest poverty rate in the nation with 27.4% of us earning less than $22,314.00 annually, which was the poverty threshold for a family of four back in 2010. They also reported that 45.8% of our children lived in poverty as opposed to only 14.5% of white children." Naturally I wanted to identify the factors that were causing these conditions, even if only to avoid the pitfalls for myself.

While discussing the topic with different people within my culture over the years, a re-occurring theme I regularly heard and still hear in the voices of many disenfranchised blacks is simply fear. It's often too easy for us to make excuses about not pursuing our dreams in life. Yet many of us will continue to do so, not realizing where the root of the problem stems from. Many times, if a positive suggestion from a friend or loved one were made to a person who needed help, more than often the attempt would be rejected.

For instance, a good friend could make a suggestion to another saying, "your smart, you should go back to school so you can make some real money doing what you love". This can be expressed in a genuine effort to help this individual. Yet more often than not, the advice will be shrugged off by that person using a host of excuses such as a lack of money, not having enough time, family issues, or sometimes all of the above.

All of which sound legitimate at first until we take a closer look at the personal habits of this individual. Upon closer examination of the issue one can't help but think, "How can he not afford to go to school or in some cases even pay child support. Yet still find spare cash to put brand new rims on his car, keep up with the latest video games, or purchase the latest pair of basketball shoes?"

Or what about that female who blames all of her issues on being a single mom who doesn't have enough time to pursue school. Although she lives only ten minutes away from the nearest community college that offers free GED classes, and online courses that eliminate the need for excessive childcare? Yet this same female will have the time and money needed to travel across town to the salon to get an overpriced hair style, head out to the night club, or even get a new tattoo to keep up with the latest styles.

Witnessing this type of behavior perplexed me even more as a youth. Why are some of us able to actively pursue our goals while others remained idle and unproductive? Some will say it's just a case of misplaced priorities and certain people are destined to dwell on the bottom of society. The idea is a bit Darwinistic, and to a point I can even agree with that kind of logic, but somehow, I felt there was more to this issue to be contemplated.

Let's take the time to break down the mentioned examples and analyze this dilemma. For instance, going back to school after a

J.G. Robinson

certain amount of years is often scary and uncertain for many people. Especially if the individual didn't perform well in class the first time around to begin with. Over time self-doubt, anxiety, and uncertainty slowly take hold in those places where logic, reason, and ambition should rule. If this continues, it won't take long for a person to doubt themselves.

What if you're the only one in the class over thirty? What if you give it your all only to fail again? How does one cope with that? In some cases, having to explain failure to everyone who supported you is often unbearable for many of us. All of these circumstances combined have effectively transformed many of the ambitious dreams our people may have had into hopeless fantasy. This often causes the original hopes of progress to be abandoned altogether.

For many of us who came from low income areas, a lack of support served as the original cause for our failures to begin with. Challenges such as these make it extremely difficult to get up the motivation required to better our lives. This in time, creates a sort of "social attrition" that is responsible for more long-term damage in our communities than most realize. Many of us already know and understand that if there's no one around to believe in us, cheer us on, or celebrate our success with, then overcoming such fear, doubt, & uncertainty by ourselves is next to impossible.

Returning to school is simply too much work for something that some believe offers little to no payoff. In the views of many, a diploma or degree is merely a piece of paper that won't guarantee us a job upon completion, nor eliminate the other discouraging factors preventing us from moving forward.

Things such as criminal records, poor credit or unpaid child support, can keep us deadlocked in poverty. A lack of an education is just "ONE" of the many factors we must deal with on a daily basis. Most of us who are dealing with these issues tend to get overwhelmed and give into our fears and doubts. This is done by coming up with suitable excuses and never trying at all.

The Black Man's Answer

Unfortunately, for some of us there are many issues that fall into this category. This is because those in low-income areas have a tendency to live fast and hard due to the circumstances surrounding our upbringing. This can cause an unusual number of mistakes to be made by the age of twenty-one. All of this is critical to understand because at a time when most people are building and setting themselves up for success in life, some of us are unwittingly doing the exact opposite.

Those living this way usually fall victim to self-destructive behavior such as dropping out of school, committing crimes, getting pregnant, or creating debt for ourselves. Therefore, when we finally do get control of ourselves and realize we want something better in life, the path that now lies before us has often become unattainable. At this point, it simply becomes easier to accept the low level of life we have become accustomed to, rather than fill ourselves with false hope trying to get something that will most likely never happen.

It's sad to say, but this kind of acceptance has become the problem. Once we have learned this type of acceptance it slowly becomes a habit. A habit that gets applied to other difficult situations we encounter throughout life. This habit is commonly referred to by others as settling or giving up.

Since we are all aware of the negative connotations that come with terms such as quitting or giving up, it should come as no surprise when we hear the excuses we do while attempting to motivate each other. I truly believe the only way to inspire our people to strive and do for self is to rid ourselves of the fear that causes these issues.

Fear causes a source of doubt, uncertainty, and ultimately the loss of a person's ability to believe in themselves. With fear even the smallest choices in life can become huge insurmountable obstacles to overcome.

Furthermore, important life decisions such as career choices that could involve relocating to a new location to start fresh, deciding to marry the person with whom we already live or have kids with, or converting to another religion because Christianity is not fulfilling us. These are all products of the same decision-making process that will sculpt a person's future. If that process is riddled with fear and self doubt, then the habit of quitting will persist, and the same ongoing cycle of poverty and ignorance will continue within the life of that individual.

If you think about it, how could anyone expect to succeed at changing their life for the better if they backed down from all the challenges and opportunities presented to them? We must understand that if we want different things in life, we must learn to do things differently. An effort must be made to reduce the amount of fear within our personal lives. Thereby creating a more positive trend of blacks that dare to dream and take full advantage of all opportunities that lie before us. Only then when we have eliminated this barrier of fear can we make room for what should be present in our decisions, which is a strong sense of self confidence!

The Answer:

We must make an effort to commit, encourage, and support each other's goals and ambitions. We must focus not on what we "think" is being supportive, but make sure we provide the assistance for those that is really needed at that particular time. This must happen especially at home within our families. Those of us who are gifted at being positive and productive should make a conscious effort to assist and empower others who seek the same. This way success becomes a reward for the group as a whole instead of the individual which encourages even more support and reinforces the need for more teamwork.

MANAGING OUR PRIDE

I honestly can't recall how many altercations I had with other young brothers as a youth growing up in my neighborhood.

However, I do remember the majority of those incidences were over small petty situations in which neither one of us wanted to back down from. At the time these altercations seemed necessary, so we didn't look weak in the eyes of our fellow peers. In each case what we stood to lose was always significantly greater than what we had to gain. In most cases the prize was bragging rights and a sense of false respect that only lasted until it was time for the next altercation.

With that being said, I feel one of our most deadly flaws as a people has to be pride. It is an overbearing, stubborn, narrow-minded way of thinking that taints the vast majority of our relationships, both romantic and otherwise. Misguided pride is present whenever our men and women don't respect each other and responsible when our people are beyond apologizing to each other. It's prevalent in families where parents don't listen to their kids and that same favor is eventually returned when the kids don't listen to the parents, and it is also a key element in prejudice and racism.

Over time, too much pride will eventually make a person uncompromising, closed minded, and ultimately ignorant. It's ok to take a certain amount of pride in who we are, where we're from, our family namesake, etc. However, if someone were to disagree with the value of any of those things or the manner in which we govern them, it should not cause anger, resentment, or hostility between one another. If so, the individual responsible for those reactions may be guilty of being too prideful.

An ordinary person absent of pride would simply regard a disagreement with another person as an unwanted comment or maybe even an unfortunate run-in with a rude person. An even better person would actually listen to the individual to figure out why such a statement was being made to begin with and determine whether or not they had a valid point.

In some cases often contrary to our own pride, we may have actually been wrong but can never muster up the strength to admit it out loud. If a comment, opinion, or action is not "intentionally" directed at us in a disrespectful manner, then there should be no

J.G. Robinson

reason to get offended. A confident person should be able to "respectfully" explain to that individual why they may want to try things a little differently in the future.

You see it's not as crucial with strangers because chances are high that we won't have to interact with them in the future. The real challenge lies with those we have to deal with on a daily basis such as friends, family, and coworkers. It is important for us to learn and develop responsible ways to resolve our differences. Safe ways that won't wreak havoc on our emotions. An inability to do so can cause our relationships to become dysfunctional and make unhappiness a reality for all who are involved.

The truth is that it's nearly impossible to reconcile problems with two individuals drunk on stubborn pride. It's not an easy step to rid ourselves of this. There are even some among us who have become too proud to work menial labor or volunteer jobs, even if that job would serve only as a temporary stepping stone for a year or two in order to achieve something greater. This has caused many missed opportunities and frustration as young blacks typically expect sufficient pay to live on from working one job and don't function well with jobs that offer only seasonal or part time employment with minimum wage salaries.

There are many of us who don't even realize how much pride has set in our spirits and personalities. In some cases, it's been a part of our sub consciousness for so long that to lose it feels like losing a dear part of who we are as an individual. You see this is the trick that pride plays on us and its one of the many reasons why we are so resistant to changing. This is because it literally feels as if we are being forced to change who we are as people. However, this is only partly true if we account for the growth and maturity that comes with defeating pride.

The truth is that to rid ourselves of excess pride is to ultimately "improve" who we are as people. We must look inward frequently on our own actions to ensure we have made the best decisions possible, and if not be fully prepared to correct it by "sincerely" apologizing when a situation has gotten out of hand.

Once we have mastered this process within ourselves a very powerful tool will have been acquired known as self-evaluation. Which if applied properly, will help increase the quality of our relationships as a whole and provide a better environment for cooperation and teamwork to flourish amongst us all in the black community.

The Answer:

We must first realize that being "independent" is not the prize we think it is. In fact, most aspects of being happy in this world require us to learn the exact opposite which is to be "dependent" on others for our well being and vice versa. According to a report done by *Black Demographics*, "marriage for instance has been a declining institution among all Americans and this decline is even more evident in our community. In 2014 only 29% of African Americans were married compared to 48% of all Americans. Half or 50% of African Americans have "never" been married compared to 33% of all Americans."

I personally believe this is because no marriage, family, or even friendship can last if the individuals in it are constantly striving to be "independent" of each other. It's one thing to build ourselves up so we aren't seen as the weak link in the chain when compared to others. It's another for the link to believe it can do it all by itself without the chain entirely.

Truthfully, the only kind of independence we should be striving for is "financial independence". This will empower us as individuals and collectively as a people by giving us the authority to govern our lands and create our own opportunities, thus granting us the control we need in our own communities. Gaining a true understanding of this will keep us from behaving in ways that are counterproductive to ourselves and our culture. All humans need to rely on each other, the sooner we acknowledge this and reduce the level pride in our

J.G. Robinson

daily interactions, the easier our lives will be.

ENVY & JEALOUSY

I remember when I was about nine years old, I used to hate it when I got a sandwich and my little sister would have to get the same thing, simply because she saw me do it. My mother would usually give into it or else my sister would have thrown a tantrum. I hated a copycat, and I still do today. "Why can't people come up with their own ideas instead of waiting around to steal someone else's?" Is what I would groan to myself while watching her skip around the room eating it with joy.

Well since then, I grew up and watched envy and jealousy take on a whole new light as I witnessed people do whatever it took to get the items or possessions held by others. This ranged anywhere from intangible desires such as respect, admiration, and fame, to tangible items such as homes, cars, or even an attractive spouse. Nothing in humanity was off limits. If the possession was coveted by one, then almost certainly there would be another who wanted the same.

Now there's nothing wrong with cherishing a few prized items that belong to us. Or wanting something nice after seeing someone else with it. In many cases this is what inspires us and gives birth to the trends and styles that become popular within our society.

However, it becomes a problem when our identity is defined by our ability, or lack thereof, to possess such things affecting how we view ourselves and treat others around us. In either case, failing to achieve these goals often causes emotional unrest in an individual. Creating issues such as depression, low self esteem, inferiority complexes, self pity, and in some cases outright anger and resentment against those who have successfully achieved the things we still long for.

Even worse are those who take action with these ill feelings as motives. Speaking against or committing acts of malice toward those who at the moment "appear" to be a bit more fortunate than ourselves. These people are known commonly in today's popular culture as "haters" the acts they commit "hating" and there is far too much of it going on in our communities for anyone successful or of a different mindset to live happily in peace amongst them.

This causes many of our young champions who may have defeated the odds of growing up in poverty and becoming statistics to seek happiness elsewhere. This consequently leaves many of our communities to continue being dominated by those plagued with feelings of hate, jealousy, envy, depression and inferiority. A perfect breeding ground to produce more of the same illnesses and perpetuate the sad cycle for future African Americans.

If we are ever going to progress pass this point we've got to make the change within ourselves to weed out jealousy and envy from our lives. This will allow us to actually encourage and support those who break the mold in our culture as opposed to criticizing or accusing them of selling out and forgetting where they came from.

The Answer:

We must stop looking to become "equal" with anyone. We must also stop looking for someone to treat us "fairly". There has never been a time or place in human history where all men have been treated as equals amongst one another, so it would be foolish for us to expect it to happen now here in America. At the end of the day the fight for "equality" has simply become the justification of "envy" in disguise.

These hidden agendas are often backed by groups of people who simply desire the same things they see others with. The concepts of receiving reparations and equality are dangerous because of this reason since they inadvertently teach that our lives are not our own to govern and imply that we cannot attain what we need to prosper on our own. These concepts also insinuate that we apparently need the existence of a superior entity to grow and find contentment.

J.G. Robinson

We have to take the time to establish our own plan to repair the damage inflicted upon our culture from slavery. Nobody cares about these issues more than us and we are definitely capable of coming together and making it happen. If we stop wasting time disagreeing amongst each other, progress will be made at an astounding rate. This is the way it has to be.

Think about it, if some group other than blacks were to assist us with gaining our much-needed progress then history would credit them as being the almighty saviors of the African American race. This could leave a bittersweet taste in our mouths, as it would still appear that we couldn't do it on our own. Let's make sure our goals are based in pure motives, so we don't fall victim to the petty bickering that comes with envy and jealousy.

HONORING OUR FAMILY HISTORY

I lived the first years of my life in a small town called Palmetto, Florida. My mother had given birth to me in her teens, and ended up dropping out of school to take care of me. My natural blood father was never a part of my life, for reasons that could only be answered by him. It was an instant formula for poverty. This became the foundation of my identity and reasons for the future choices I would be faced with in the years to come.

Unfortunately, there is nothing special or unique about my situation. I have ran into countless numbers of our people with similar or even worse beginnings than myself. The question for most is, how does one salvage something special worth cherishing from a situation that had nothing worthy of respect in it to begin with?

The primary building block of any person or culture is the knowledge of their own history. It is often said that "whoever controls the past, also controls the future". I find there to be truth in this statement. We need to know where we've been in order to know where we are going. We need to embrace not only our ancient African ancestry but our immediate American family history as well. It establishes value and respect for who we and our families are in this world and what it took to get us here.

With this knowledge we become able to form newfound family traditions. This is important because tradition is a vital part of any culture. Any tradition formed without historic significance will be short lived. Many of us have lost all connection or knowledge with anyone of great grandparent status or higher. Even when we do have the information it typically only comes from one side of the family, which is only half of the story of who we are. This information is critical as it provides the most recent explanation to our current positions in life.

If your grandfather was the first to own land in your family, use that as inspiration to do the same. If your great aunt used to run a successful business downtown, keep it going and inform your kids that good business runs in the family. If you have an ancestor who fought in the Civil War, honor their memory and teach to your future generations that your family "directly" fought for our freedom here in America and make a point to mention it come Veterans Day, Memorial Day, and any other time someone questions our status in this country.

Our failures have value as well. We should use the pain of those who were sent to prison for life, lynched by the clan, had kids taken by the state, or strung out on drugs, as an ever-present reminder of what can happen to us if we choose to live an unrighteous life.

We should also learn the meaning and history of our last names and make a conscious decision on whether or not to keep them for our future generations. Whatever the story may be, good or bad, we must take the time to honor the "struggle" made by those before us. As well as admiring those of us who are still living the struggle today.

J.G. Robinson

Let's document the trials and accomplishments of each other as well, since our fight today will be the story of our children's tomorrow. This way we can reduce the amount of us who may be wandering through life with no sense of belonging, and effectively rebuild our culture and racial sense of identity. This in time should reduce the amount of us who believe that our lives would be better spent mixed amongst the other cultures.

The Answer:

The honoring of African American family history must become a priority for us all until it becomes a routine habit for us to preserve it naturally. It should eventually become something we are known for doing as a people, like a new stereotype of sorts. According to information published by the *National Kids Count,* "young black kids have the highest percentage of being from single parent homes at over 60% percent from 2011 – 2015."

This makes knowledge of our family history even more important as over half of us are probably wondering about the side of the family tree we rarely got to see or interact with. No one is going to cherish our lineage more than we do, and likewise no one will tell or portray the story of our people in the history books or theaters better than we can to each other. Therefore we must take the reins and guide our history in the manner we see fit.

AFFIRMING OUR PERSONAL IDENTITY

I believe I was in first or second grade when I became conscious of "who I am" as an individual. In school I would see other children with their parents, speaking different languages, dressing different, even practicing different religions. I started asking my mom questions like, "Why is my name James?" and "Why do we have

Christmas and not Hanukkah?" I also asked, "Are we really from Africa, and if so can we go back?" There were even times where I'd asked if we still had family over there. These are probably the same typical naïve questions that many black youths have once they become aware of themselves.

However, it's important to know this is a very crucial time in forming the psyche of an individual. What we say to our children during this time can potentially lay the foundation for years to come in regards of how they view themselves. So, it's important our parents and elders have a certain amount of wisdom and guidance to offer during this time period. A lack of proper guidance for children in our culture typically occurs when child birth happens at an unusually early age in a couple's life. This condition is often made worse when combined with the absence of a parent.

Obviously not much wisdom could be bestowed upon a child by the parents if they are technically still considered kids themselves. It's even worse if the child in question is placed in foster care and moved from home to home with different guardians. This also can be a problem with those who have been adopted by individuals who aren't of the same culture. It's great to have a stable home and a person that cares for you when being adopted, nobody will deny that. However, there may be serious identity gaps in how that child views themselves as opposed to how the rest of society perceives them.

For instance, my wife and I have a stable home environment and could adopt a child if we so desired, but how fair would it be for us to adopt a young girl of another culture? Especially if we knew only our own culture as African Americans? The child would end up being raised eating traditional soul food, attending black churches, listening to Reggae, Hip-Hop, R&B, Gospel music, and so on, because this is the kind of life my wife and I live.

Yes, she would be loved by us like one of our own, but would that be enough? Especially when there are so many black children out there who need a home that would fit so much easier? Now I'm not saying that only adopted kids can have these issues, but refusal

J.G. Robinson

to acknowledge these things could wreak havoc on an individual's identity. It's also been stated by many experts that kids with identity issues tend to have a higher propensity to use drugs, suffer from depression, and in some cases even commit suicide.

As African Americans there are many instances where our "blackness" can come into question not only by those outside the race but more often by other fellow African Americans or blacks of different nationalities. It is important for us to remember we are "people" first, and as a person we have the right to be as unique or common as we'd like to be.

Furthermore, we also reserve the right to change our mind if we so desire. Meaning there is no imaginary box our behavior can be forced into. We can listen to gangster rap today, and attend an opera show with our friends tomorrow. We can learn to speak Japanese and continue living in the projects. We can be NASCAR fans, while wearing sagging pants and a head full of dreadlocks.

We can convert to Buddhism, and pickup snowboarding on the weekends. We can move to Russia and still dine on collard greens and smoked neck bones. We can be half white and still become the first Black President of the United States. We have no limitations! As long as our ideals are legal and morally sound we can strive for whatever our hearts desire.

We must not ever allow anyone to make us feel inadequate or self conscious about how we live our lives or the values taught to our children. Establishing this state of mind allows us to effectively and confidently explain our position to those who are usually ignorant or close minded about cultural issues. The ability to defend our own personal views and actions against each other is a skill that shouldn't be needed but unfortunately, it's often those closest to us that require the most understanding.

We all know that certain mother or grandparent who won't even think of their child considering any religion other than "Christianity" in their life. We also know of that wife who looks at you in horror should you ever suggest moving to another country, or anywhere for that matter that's not predominantly black or close to family. Many of us have likewise experienced that "non-black" co-worker who insists on "bumping fists" every day at work in some half-hearted attempt to display to us and others that he is "down with blacks", when we all know a simple handshake or hello would suffice.

Those of us who have dated outside the race know that certain "look" we get from certain friends or relatives of our "non-black" lovers when we were introduced to them for the first time and they realized we were different. Finally, is that fellow African American coworker who believes we should have each other's back although you don't know, like, or respect anything about them.

Unfortunately, these situations are all too common in our lives and typically have the potential to cause unnecessary stress if not handled properly. It may be due to the side effects of integration and the illusion of the "melting pot" ideal, but it seems many of us are divided and confused on what our cultural identity should be now more than ever. I personally can say I have met very few black families who seriously practice or celebrate the tradition of Kwanzaa for instance. Issues such as this cause me to ask myself, "what is our official position on this topic?"

It seems many of us out there are not sure whether to push hard for blackness or to blend in with popular mainstream American culture. I consequently feel there are many who misinterpret or overcomplicate the issue of our identity because they share valued relationships with friends or lovers of another race. These bonds typically prompt them to use phrases such as "I don't see color", or "We all bleed red at the end of the day", as neutral statements that allow them to keep from fully identifying themselves with any "one" particular race or culture.

In my experience there are only two real factors that should determine a person's cultural allegiance. The first lies within whom they share their blood with when it comes time to marry and reproduce. The second is who they choose to disburse their wealth with through the course of their life, especially when it comes to things such as inheritances. Everything else is just normal human interaction in which we are all free to do as we please.

I believe this to be a good indicator of who we can trust to be genuine in their actions and motives. It can also serve as a good principle to be taught to our people and be used as an identifier. This would be helpful when the time comes to distinguish who is a friend of the culture and who is not.

This would be especially useful in the case of evaluating politicians, researching businesses, and networking with other organizations that are out there in our communities. In time, if done properly this will strengthen the sense of identity within each of us and teach the overall concept of self-awareness to those who are willing to seek it.

The Answer:

We should stop worrying about how the entire race is perceived as a whole. We didn't all agree during the civil rights movement, and even in Africa our ancestors had (and still have) many different tribes all with different cultures, and dialects. Somehow here in America we've been led to believe we all should act and behave the same as well as think on one accord.

Only bloodshed and warfare has ever been able to force change on an entire race of people and we are in no position to do that, to ourselves or anyone else. Instead we need to focus on our individual families and communities first.

Our men should focus on becoming strong intelligent leaders and providers, with an unending sense of order and wisdom. Our women should do the same with an emphasis on compassion and understanding. Then once we have achieved stability we can come together and improve our families one household at a time. This will profoundly establish our own personal identities since safe and secure families can't help but produce better well-rounded people.

Chapter 2

Culture

RACIAL HISTORY

One disheartening thing I remember experiencing as a young black male growing up was the lack of information regarding our history. There was not much to be offered in the school library pertaining to black culture and my family members themselves only knew but so much. My mother had grown up during the sixties and seventies and could tell me about her memories of desegregation.

She could speak about having to endure the process of changing schools during that time, but that's about it. Now that I think about it, there were very few folks I can remember who even tried to speak of anything black that predated our time here in America.

As a child I remember being captivated by the story of King Chaka Zulu when it was aired on television back then played marvelously by actor Henry Cele. It was an intoxicating tale of revenge, power, destiny, and better than anything it was actually based on true life accounts. I couldn't get enough of it. It was like giving a glass of ice cold sparkling water to someone who had been wandering through the unrelenting heat of the desert. Finally, I had come across factual events of a real life black man who rose to become King of his own people in Southern Africa.

This was profound to me because I'd always heard it said in our culture from those looking to empower us, how we were a race of Kings and Queens, but until then I'd never had any evidence or references to look back upon to see if that were true. At a certain point I had begun to wonder if it was even true at all, or if it was just wishful thinking on our part. Perhaps a simple source of motivation and encouragement for our people during hard times. You can imagine my delight to find out that there was truth behind the tales and that they weren't just empty sentiments.

J.G. Robinson

My perspective changed greatly in how I viewed myself and my people. I only wished to dig deeper and find more of what I didn't know concerning us and share the same experiences with others who sought the same. However, that's where it became tricky. I began to realize not everyone cared about their own history, or any history at all for that matter.

There were many who saw the information, shrugged their shoulders and moved on. They did not possess the same passion and desire I did to discover more about their own lineage. It was then that I began to realize not everyone has the same roles in the fight for progress amongst our people.

What I did come to understand with time, is that it's worth the effort to make as many as we can aware of themselves as possible. It was something that would be beneficial to all. Now whether they learned to apply the information and put it into action is up to them.

It's no secret the African American people have a history of slavery in this country, I think we all know that by now. However, the problem I've found is with most individuals, (of all races) it seems as if that's where the knowledge begins and ends with us here in America. Few are able to expand beyond that range and provide "factual history" concerning us. For many it's almost as if we don't even have a history until slavery began, and anything before that is considered to be traditional "African" history which we somehow aren't a part of.

This is a problem, not only does this hinder us from identifying ourselves internationally with our ancestral homelands, but it furthermore causes us to disassociate with blacks from other regions as well. Therefore, many of us remain divided as strangers rather than coming together like the distant relatives we truly are.

The Answer:

It is possible to reach back to the motherland to explore and rediscover the rich culture lost from our original homelands. We can research the different foods, languages, and traditions still held by

The Black Man's Answer

many tribes existing today. We can then incorporate this knowledge and distribute it in places like prestigious black universities for example to help educate the youth.

Thanks to new technology such as DNA testing. Many have been able to genetically isolate the region from which their ancestors dwelled. Once satisfactory knowledge has been gained of our past culture, we can then merge and reinforce the old ways with our new ways here in America. This will allow us to practice them in our churches and other black owned facilities.

Over time, the traditions would gradually blend into our identities as African Americans and create a new sense of self entirely. This would give us some common ground with our brethren within the many nations of Africa, as well as strengthening our culture here in America.

DEALING WITH POPULAR CULTURE

Mainstream media and entertainment have no doubt influenced much of our society here in America. In fact, there are many who believe it has surpassed religion as being the dominating factor in our life decisions. This means a large majority of people in today's society will base weddings, careers, traditions, and behavior within their homes, off something seen on television rather than biblical scripture or cultural tradition. This could be a valid point as I've personally witnessed in many low income black communities, a decrease in the practice of traditions and an ever growing rise in trends and fads.

It's not uncommon to find our youth utilizing whatever provocative notions seen on television as a replacement for their culture. Habits we thought were going to wear off and eventually fade away have begun to last for generations now. Trends such as sagging the pants, dealing in drugs, and even gang culture can now in some instances can be traced from father to son.

Phrases used in everyday rap lyrics have become common punch lines for Americans when referencing our culture. All of these factors combined have mentally taken a toll on many (including us) as to what the image and perceptions of a black man and woman could be in modern day America.

It would be nice if we could produce a more positive and wholesome image for ourselves here and abroad internationally. Many cultures out there learn far more about African American culture through television and music than they will ever actually ask us to our face.

It would be to our benefit if there were more positive elements of our culture out there for others to experience. The most important thing we could improve upon to do this is increase our influence and control over the media that currently exists. This would make sure the images displayed concerning us meet our approval.

However, we would have to "live" that change in order for others to accept it as truth and it takes all of us to make that happen. Much of what's marketed concerning our culture is one dimensional, meaning it only depicts us in a certain view. Therefore, we have to make sure we encompass as many different aspects of who we are as a people in order to transcend the current stigma that many refuse to admit still exist today concerning us.

One good place to start is with entertainment. Many of us have transcended the barriers for our people by doing well in the entertainment industry. There are some who even have the creative control to influence exactly what is put out, whether it be in movies, books, sports, performing arts, or music. This is fantastic because it's not uncommon for many of the products produced by the entertainment industry regarding African Americans to be filled with drama.

Let's take our music for instance, when it comes to R&B music a large percentage of it used to represent love, and was the kind of stuff many liked to hear played around family, weddings, and in some cases even funerals. These days what remains of the R&B music genre is consumed with references and innuendos to "SEX" rather than love. Furthermore, those who sing it are required to be young, cool, and attractive so they can come across as adequate representatives of the sex filled messages they portray to society.

Others subscribe to the "heartache" versions of the music that focuses primarily on failed love and relationships. These songs tend to go on and on either complaining about their "failed relationships" or apologizing for being the one who caused it to fail with their inconsiderate actions to begin with.

This reflects the emotional pity party that many go through on an everyday basis. I feel only a small percentage of R&B represents pure love, happiness, and soul that all can respect and enjoy. Unfortunately, this is also the type of R&B that typically has the lowest sales in the industry.

The same can be found in Rap music. Once upon a time Rap music was a new innovative sound and way for our people to express ourselves artistically. Brand new techniques were invented such as break dancing and scratching on turntables. There was no violence, drugs, or disrespect associated with it. Typically, if you heard it coming from a home in the neighborhood you knew someone was having a good time.

These days what we have left in Hip-Hop music are the misconstrued imitations of those who originally pioneered it. It has become a genre filled with the voices of many who are lost, angry, confused, or misguided due to their various situations in life. Some of them are disgruntle and create songs full of anger and street violence. There are some who claim gang affiliation just to gain street credibility and sell a record. There are also those out there who just want to party, get high, or do the latest dance.

Then there is the last percentage that belongs to the conscious rap community. This type of Rap usually has a great message, but is often too political to get sufficient radio play or draw crowds at a night club for most to care. Therefore, conscious rap doesn't sell as well and the industry remains dominated by the lesser two categories.

At this stage in the game I feel that very little of Rap is unique or innovative anymore, and many who are associated with it don't have any true musical talent. Most only seek fortune and fame as a ticket to an easier life, but don't really know how to respect the concept of musicianship within itself. This explains why the quality and reputation of the music has decreased because in many cases the people making it aren't musicians at all. Some of them don't know a thing about reading musical notes, songwriting, or even how to play an instrument.

Let's also take a look at our representation in modern day literature. I personally have always loved to read and write, but as time went along I noticed there seemed to be certain unspoken boundaries on what a black person was able to be an authority on in the world of literature. It seemed as if we were widely and easily accepted as long as the topics we wrote upon were neutral or harmless in nature such as a cookbook for instance.

I noticed it was much easier for me to find a book by us on how to properly prepare soul food than it was to find a book about a black scientist that pioneered his own research in Bio-Mechanics or find ground breaking theories from a black philosopher who changed the way we viewed life itself.

Furthermore, even if you did manage to find these rare authors, the book typically would not be listed in the African American section. You'd have to go elsewhere to that particular field of study for that. This perplexed me because it made me feel as though I had to write about a certain topic in order to get placed in a certain genre of books. Otherwise I would have to search through all the titles just to find out who the authors were in that particular category. This also caused me to ponder why just "these" books were considered to be African American literature?

If a white doctor for instance published his lifelong research on the health of black women from his thirty years of medical practice in southern Mississippi, was that research not pertinent to our community? I'd hate to miss out on some good information about my people just because it wasn't done "exclusively" by African American authors. So, I really began to question the system that was responsible for making these decisions.

These days things have changed a bit from when I was growing up. I can hardly find an "African American section" at all in most book stores anymore. Most have given it a watered-down title such as "cultural studies" that encompasses the works of several different ethnicities as opposed to just black literature by itself.

I mentioned those previous scenarios to demonstrate my perspective on these issues, but there are many more instances that could be brought up concerning sports, movies, and theatre as well. The bottom line is we must actively monitor what messages get produced concerning us. If some are found to be unfavorable we must also make sure we take whatever action necessary to reduce the negative impact of it on our community.

The Answer:

An effort must be made to increase the amount of reliable media sources within our community. A huge majority of the media we subscribe to is still primarily owned by others outside of our culture. This causes what little media we do produce to meet the approval of others before we can release it out unto our own.

According to information published in the _Washington Post_, "in August of 2015 blacks only owned a total of 10 television stations." We have to take this into account, so we can establish additional means of communicating that don't allow others to censor what we say. Only then can we stop relying on others to tell us what is going on with each other and our homeland as well as other black issues abroad.

J.G. Robinson

ESTABLISHING TRADITION

As a young man growing up in my youth, one thing I've always felt our culture could use a lot more of is meaningful tradition. It may seem small, insignificant, and to some even trivial. Yet I believe it serves as a vital source of pride and value in a person's culture. I have noticed over the years as I traveled how special these occasions are for people.

For instance, there is something special about a young Jewish boy celebrating his Bar mitzvah. Or a young Latina girl enjoying her Quinceanera. As a people I feel most African Americans have very few if any of these events for ourselves. I personally believe establishing our own set of traditions for our culture would have a significant effect in the long run concerning how our future generations would view themselves and our culture.

As the adult males in our communities we should take the time to establish different rites of passage into manhood for our sons. Our women should also implement events that celebrate a young woman's virtue, as well as her transition into womanhood. We can also develop cherished family heirlooms that would travel within our family bloodlines for many generations to come.

I personally believe achieving small milestones such as these in our households would keep us one step closer to maintaining a sense of love, unity, and happiness. It would also provide more reasons for the family to come together and celebrate each other's worth and value.

For a long time simply surviving poverty was the primary concern in the lives of many African Americans. This over time caused other important needs such as financial recovery and cultural reconstruction to give way to attaining the basics such as food, clothes, shelter, and education. There are those of us who have succeeded at establishing a middle-class lifestyle amongst ourselves.

The Black Man's Answer

However, I personally feel little has been done to fill the void in our culture created from slavery and years of systematic oppression. Some of us have unwittingly made American popular culture our new way of life. There are many of us who conform to society's loose moral values, and "watered down" traditions.

A common example can be seen when we celebrate holidays with pagan or unknown origins such as Halloween or Valentine's day that hardly have a solid foundation in our culture or history to begin with.

The Answer:

If positive steps are taken to introduce sound values and traditions into our community, then I believe our people would accept them. We must take the time to produce and present such ceremonies and symbolism at our places of worship, family reunions, and community functions.

Something as simple as holding a clenched fist in the air for ten seconds of silence for our fallen ancestors can become a powerful symbol if done with meaning. It can take place ceremonially at the end or at the beginning of our events. Similar to the way the national anthem is played before all major sporting events. These are the kind of things we must begin to incorporate on our own to give our people a better sense of culture and togetherness.

LANGUAGE

In today's culture I have experienced that many of us tend to judge each other based on our use of the language. As a southern black male, I personally felt the sting of judgment when I first traveled to New York City back in the summer of 1997. I was referred to as a "BAMMA" and told to "stop speaking so country" by several of the young blacks of that region.

J.G. Robinson

At the time being only nineteen years old, I never even realized I spoke with a southern drawl. Everyone I knew back home spoke like me, everyone that was black anyway. So I began to ask myself, "did I pass judgment on my people this way as well?" The truth was yes, I did, and still do.

I remember back then blacks who spoke English too properly were suspected as "sell outs" who thought they were better than me. This idea usually remained that way until they proved otherwise. Furthermore, blacks who spoke with a certain southern slang were usually accepted as my folk unless it was revealed they couldn't be trusted.

This phenomenon manifests itself in other ways in society as well. It shows up in everyday tasks such as participating in job interviews, public speaking, dating, and court appearances. All are examples of instances that leave us open to judgment in which language can be a huge factor. Often our language in the streets can be excessive containing profanity and slang.

It's not uncommon for some of us to come across as aggressive, argumentative, or unnecessarily loud when speaking as well. I feel this can be attributed to a mixture of poor etiquette and bad habits. This possibly stems from the fact that a significant percentage of our people have spent some time in correctional facilities or low-income housing projects. These are places that tend to possess an unusually high amount of impoverished and less educated blacks.

Since many of us have had unfortunate run-ins with the law, the attitudes needed for surviving in prison have undoubtedly trickled back into the street which is usually where we run into the gang, pimp, and drug dealing mentalities. This inevitably causes the behavior we deem as being "ghetto", "street", "ignorant" or just plain old "criminal".

This is also the same energy many Rap and Hip-Hop artists tap into and convey through lyric and song. It's not uncommon for an entertainer to glamorize things in their music that are heinous in nature which is referred to as having "street credibility".

The Black Man's Answer

Unfortunately, the side effects of this has caused many of our youth to place far too much pride in being from the streets. It's also not uncommon for them to use what some refer to as Ebonics to express themselves and communicate out in mainstream society.

Most African Americans do not possess the native tongues of our ancestors. We only know how to speak English as our primary and often sole language. I have found that many of us aren't sure how to feel about this situation. It is somewhat similar to the Christian religion which also became something that was inherited and blindly passed from generation to generation.

I feel this is a problem because now we've come from not being able to communicate with our African brethren, to literally sharing the culture of those who were guilty of enslaving and oppressing us. I furthermore feel the reason why it's so prevalent to see backs who intermarry with whites is because our cultures are so similar!

Other ethnicities who've kept their native tongues and culture don't intermarry with blacks nearly as often as we do into white American culture. I feel this is because we commonly share the same religion, language, and history with each other so many don't see any problem with sharing the same household as well.

Thanks to slavery we are now two different races of people with one very similar history and culture between us. This is why many find it foolish to consider that blacks and whites have any differences in this country at all, and to be honest the way things are right now, they're probably right. Both of our races have far more things in common than we have that's different from one another. This by itself is causing great confusion as to where our loyalties should be placed.

Now I don't attribute our current condition all solely on speaking different languages. I do however, want to point out that it does make a significant difference in how easy it is for two people to come together. Don't believe me? Well let's try this, close your eyes and think for a second of how many married couples you've met that were Russian and Jamaican for instance? Or Arab and Mexican?

J.G. Robinson

Or even couples who were just dating where one was from India and the other Korean? Or how about an Ethiopian man who was married to a Japanese woman? I'm sure there's a few exceptions out there for each, but you won't have nearly as many examples to choose from as you do between the black and white races found right here in America.

The reason you don't see these examples is because their cultures are simply too far apart, and I don't just mean distance. I am speaking of language, culture, and religion combined. These differences make for quite a fearsome barrier, so even if two people are physically attracted to one another it's often not enough. Now on the other hand let's think about the interracial black and white relationships witnessed here in America. It's not hard at all to bridge the gap between two English speaking, often Christian, Americans now is it?

The question many will ask today is, "What's so bad about that?" They will follow up by saying, "Isn't it a good thing that we are blending together and becoming a true melting pot? In fact, isn't that what Martin's dream was all about?" If this is your way of thinking, then you are already lost.

Martin wanted equal opportunity and fair treatment of his people by the American government under the constitution they claimed to serve, nothing less. He saw integration as a way to achieve that goal. However, he never wanted his fellow African Americans to lose their identity as a people and completely subscribe and conform to white culture and all of its ills.

This was more of an unanticipated side effect rather than a goal. It's also important for us to remember that integration was merely the "first phase" of Martins plan. He never expected integration by itself to be the cure for everything wrong in the black community. It was however a vital necessary first step in his vision for equality. Unfortunately, due to his untimely death, we never got to see the rest of his plan unfold.

For a race of people language can be a great identifier. Without this we will constantly struggle to find ways to separate ourselves from the other cultures in this country. Hence the elaborate names given to some of our children that are often neither African, English, nor Christian in meaning or origin.

I believe this directly reflects our own self-conscious desire to obtain separate identities not just for ourselves, but for our children and future generations as well. It's time we address why this happens, the issue of language, and the perceptions it gives us within our society.

The Answer:

Speaking proper English is great. It often displays to others we possess a sharp and functioning mind regardless of what our educational level or financial status may be. Many from other cultures have their native tongue to fall back on. In the case of many white Americans, English "is" the tongue of their ancestors, so they speak it freely and proudly.

Their culture also publishes dictionaries that define which words will or won't exist in their English language for the rest of us who speak it. I propose we here in America re-establish a link with several nations of Africa and pick one or two dialects worthy of assimilating back into our culture here in America.

Over time as different foods, events, music, dances, colloquialisms, and customs get created, we can slowly begin issuing these items names in the new chosen language. Then we can start integrating them within our existing culture. I think if done properly we will begin to replace much of the sense of culture we are missing here in this country.

The truth is Dr. Martin Luther King already proved integration can be done, as we've done it here with white Americans. Now that we have a working blueprint for it, there is absolutely no reason why we can't take the time to re-integrate back within the roots of our own African ancestry.

RELIGION

It's common knowledge most African Americans have inherited the religion of Christianity imposed on our ancestors from slavery days. This has for many caused a void amongst our spiritual beliefs and cultural identity. The inevitable question of what our true religion was before the oppression of our ancestors and why don't we go back to it, must be answered.

This is a question often asked by our youth, and seldom answered by our elders. If you were like me, when you asked the tough questions about God your folks probably wrote you off as being young and foolish, and continued to praise the lord the same as they always did. This usually left you with no real course of action but to keep quiet and blindly follow the herd.

Most don't realize that doing this often causes a child's faith to be placed more in the people guiding them, then in the actual teachings of the religion itself. This is why it's so hard for many to continue the practice of going to church once they mature since they never had true faith in it to begin with. Many kids end up simply following the church crowd and doing whatever it takes to earn the approval of their elders. However, once they mature and no longer require the approval of their elders, so goes their need to attend church as well.

Many are aware of this and how it continues to be the unspoken "elephant in the room", of our people's faith. To question the faith is not only seen as a sign of disrespect for the word of God, but also to our family members who live by it as well. Therefore, inevitably the faith of Christianity is practiced and enforced regardless of what we may think or feel.

I have found in some cases that "blind" obedience to Christianity tends to act more as a communication barrier between our generations rather than the spiritual beacon of guidance it should be. We must not be afraid to research and explore the true faith of our people before committing to what American society has presented to us.

I suggest taking the time to explore all spiritual aspects of this world first before settling on a faith that you plan to practice for the rest of your life and introduce to your children. This way we can make a clear "educated" decision on what our faith should be and if our people still choose to become Christians and pass it down, then so be it. At least then, we will have confidently chosen our faith out of knowledge and awareness instead of oppression and ignorance.

Once we have properly researched and exhausted all possible options of what other religions and beliefs can provide, may we satisfy our souls and spirits by choosing what our hearts desire to worship. There still may be some who choose not to worship at all. In any case this coupled with an educated mind of our own free will should allow us to make a secure decision which is the way it should be. Then our legacy will no longer be that we were forced or peer pressured into believing it by our loved ones or oppressors. Nor will it be that we simply spoon-fed it to the next generation of our children without logic or reasoning.

The Answer:

I truly believe it would be a great thing to make the church the leader of social change again in our communities. Good networking such as partnering with local police, the city council, local courts, and other powers in the city to reduce situations like crime and poverty. Also, the church has the ability to work with schools, and other youth programs in the area to create scholarships for those who show potential in their congregation.

I've even heard of some ministries being strong and resourceful enough to create shelters, food banks, and other social programs for those who have fallen on hard times. There are some churches out there who are doing a fantastic job on these things. Unfortunately,

J.G. Robinson

there are also those who aren't. If enough churches seriously committed to doing more for the "communities" of their members, the church would regain its respect in the culture that it enjoyed once before.

With that being said, whether it's a church, mosque, or a temple, we should all be able to appreciate anything that brings peace, unity, and more positive strength to our community.

THE CONSCIOUS BLACK COMMUNITY

Since the emancipation of blacks in America many have attempted to organize and lead our people to a higher state of existence. Organizations such as the U.N.I.A, the Nation of Islam, the Black Panthers, the Five Percenters, and the Black Israelites to name a few. Today there are still many different groups of African Americans out there who claim to be able to remove the invisible shackles of oppression and inequality that still plague our communities. Some swear to be able to do it by religion, others by knowledge, historical research, government secrets, or all the above.

Personally, I don't have anything against any of the groups out there who are actively trying to make a positive change for us in our communities. I would only advise our people to take caution in accepting the teachings of some of these groups since certain organizations may not have the best interest of our people at heart.

In some cases, their hearts are in the right place, but their methods may be impractical or ineffective. A good way to determine this is to simply ask ourselves or someone who is already involved in the organization this simple question, "will being a part of this organization improve my life or the condition of my community?" If the answer is yes, then have them explain how.

Often you will find they are either talking about issues that matter only to them, or that many of the issues they claim to assist you with can be achieved on your own without the extra efforts they are requesting from you. If the answer is no, then it's obvious you may want to move on.

Another way to determine an organization's worth is by analyzing their use of time and money. These are two of the most valuable resources known to man. If your organization constantly takes them from you and never replaces them, you may want to reevaluate why you even need them to begin with.

When dealing with a new group or entity. Money should not always have to flow out from your account, occasionally they should be helping the money flow back in! They should be able to provide services that involve everyone coming together to do things like keeping a fellow member's family from being evicted or getting their car repossessed during hard times. Similar to the way a "union" claims to protect its members.

In short, if we are spending our time, energy, and money with an organization, then there should be some hardcore **BENEFITS** we should expect to receive for doing so! Benefits such as programs that assist with the cost of groceries, or the cost of daycare for those who need it. To uplift our community is to look out for us all, "especially" those of us who are already committed to the cause. Think about it, how can anyone save or enlighten the entire black race when they can't even watch over the few in their own neighborhood?

Unfortunately, it's not uncommon for many of these groups to lose sight of that and become yet another entity draining money, hope, and energy out of an already exhausted community. It's also important to note that these organizations may have hidden agendas of their own. So let's be careful to do our research before joining just anyone. The line between black unity and black supremacy can be very fine in many people's eyes. Let's make sure we remain on the side that benefits "all" of our people instead of a few.

J.G. Robinson

The Answer:

As a black man, I like to learn about the history of the Moors and romanticize ancient Egypt and other wonders of Africa as much as anyone. However, that alone will never bring progress to our people. To those of us who consider themselves to be conscious minded, please know that educating the rest of us on our history is great but what most of us really need is financial help.

We need reliable funding and responsible people to assist in the administering of those funds to facilitate the improvement of our schools, streets, homes, healthcare, and employment. Any group who can provide us with that kind of assistance is definitely worth the attention of our people.

Chapter 3
Respect

GENERAL RESPECT

Everyone is entitled to a certain amount of respect regardless of race, age, culture, gender, religious creed, annual income, etc. As the saying goes we should "treat others as you would treat yourself." However, everyone is human and from time to time a situation will occur in which we all will experience disrespectful behavior in one way or another.

In our culture it's not uncommon for these incidences to get out of hand and become violent. In my experience these confrontations tend to occur more frequently in poor under privileged communities. In some cases the consequences of these aggressive confrontations are often drastic and in some cases even fatal.

I've also witnessed in many cases how the person who is the bigger aggressor even gains respect not necessarily because he or she was right, but because they won the fight. This mentality has produced toxic results in our society because now we have individuals who base respect off violence, and do so instead of using words to command respect or settle disagreements.

There are some of us out in society who must learn how to use words to express ourselves and resolve our differences. If not, we otherwise could resort to those same tactics of confrontation and intimidation when issues of disrespect arise. If these habits continue, they end up being the only manner in which we know how to communicate with others.

This issue could occur with anyone we know from strangers to our loved ones such as spouses, siblings, or our children. This is a dynamic that plays a role in many of our domestic violence cases. Let's stop promoting this type of behavior as it contributes to poor

J.G. Robinson

relationships. It's better that we focus on learning healthier ways to interact with each other.

The Answer:

These days the smallest act of violence upon another person can get you convicted of assault, domestic violence, or even child abuse. The law has no sympathy for physical violence of any kind, and our people are paying a high price for it with felonies, loss of rights, custody of kids, incarceration, and in some cases even death.

Let's learn to congratulate those who've mastered the spoken word and frown upon those who resort to fighting to solve issues. We should also begin to honor and appreciate those in our culture who can keep calm in stressful situations and articulate their grievances rather than admiring those who get loud and irate just to prove a point.

Peer pressure can be used for positive goals as well as negative ones. Let's strive to improve this ability. I believe if done correctly, we would gain much respect for our culture. Also, from those who would observe our conflict resolution skills from afar.

RESPECT FOR OUR FAMILY MEMBERS

We often take for granted the ones we should treasure the most, our family members. Unfortunately, a lack of respect for them typically occurs because some of us have experienced that our family members can be just as deceitful as a complete stranger off the street.

This realization causes many of us to harbor distrust for our relatives as well. This is damaging to an individual as the absence of a good family foundation leaves us with no support structure for the challenges that lie ahead in our lives. There are many who can voice how false hopes and hurt feelings run rampant in our communities because of the things they've had said or done to them by their so-called beloved family members.

Sadly, I have found very few people with bad blood within their family, who are able to truly forgive and fight to preserve the black family as a whole. It's almost as if their loss of trust in family, caused a lack of trust in the race as well.

There are a lot of false "Cosby Show" like expectations out there regarding how our families should be. These ideals aren't realistic for most people and tend to cause unneeded stress for ourselves and our loved ones who are trying to live up to it. When those expectations aren't met many of us feel hurt, cheated, let down, and sometimes even betrayed.

If an act was criminal in nature towards us, the fact that it was our own flesh and blood who committed the offense can make it down right unforgivable. This causes many to break their bond with their loved ones out of distrust and in some cases, completely end the relationship altogether.

Everyone has to trust, depend, or rely on someone to make it in this world. It's imperative we don't misjudge the potential that a strong family can have in our lives. It can directly impact our level of happiness. We must also get back to honoring our elders with respect as well as our children.

Our grandparents may not be able to do the things they used to, but we must never forget they got us where we are, so we have to treat them accordingly. We must try our best not to throw them in a nursing home at the first inconvenience they bring our way.

If over time it becomes necessary that we must place them in a home, then we should also take the time to visit them regularly and be concerned about their well being in their last days. We should never just abandon them at the facility and show up only once or twice a year, just to ease our own conscience in order to feel better about the situation.

J.G. Robinson

The same can be said for our children. It is a blessing to have happy healthy children running around in our likeness. We should never neglect our kids. If we weren't ready for them to be in our lives that is the fault of the parents not the child. There are too many cases where our kids pay the price for their parent's lack of planning or understanding.

We should take the time to listen and tell them we love them more often than many of us do. It's understandable there may be a time when finances are tight and earning a living and providing for your children takes priority over all. However, affection and compliments have always been free, so there's no excuse not to give those to our children no matter what the scenario is!

Our communities must not forget this, and we must express our love regularly to our kids because when it comes to family, the day will come when we will need it back in return.

The Answer:

First things first, we have to understand what a family is, and why it's important to maintain one. This is something I feel some of us in this culture have never really comprehended to begin with. As stated previously, there are those of us who base our concept of what a family should be off of television shows. You see it's hard to show proper respect and appreciation for something when you're not even sure if you ever properly received it to begin with.

Whether or not our ideas are realistic of what a family should be is a question we all need to ask ourselves and come to a conclusion on before we can hope to accomplish the goal of creating a healthy functional family for ourselves and children.

It would also help if we could be sure to pick some reasonable real-life examples of people we knew to measure ourselves and loved ones to when trying to determine the proper build of a family. Instead of comparing others to fictional characters we've seen on television or possibly read in our favorite novels. This way if we can't find a few examples of the relationships we seek in real life, then our expectations may be too high and a little unfair to expect from our loved ones. In some cases, we may even have to have a slice of "humble pie" and understand they aren't a hundred percent pleased with the roles we play in their lives either, but they make it work!

It would also be a big help if we did not put our family members on pedestals. Yes, they share our DNA, and we care so much more for them than we do others we don't know. However, in the end they are just average people just like anyone else and they are going to make the same mistakes everyone else does.

It's more important we understand this when they mess up, and acknowledge that they need our forgiveness, patience, and understanding. These positive factors resonate much more so than our harsh criticism and judgment. If that's all they receive from us when things are tough, how can we expect any different from them in our low moments when we need the same?

PROFESSIONAL RESPECT

I got my first job when I was thirteen years old. It wasn't much, I pulled weeds and cleaned classrooms at a vocational school for $4.25 an hour. Even back then most folks made more per hour than I did, but to me my little paycheck meant the world. It was the first time I earned money, punched a clock, or had to cash a paycheck. It taught me a lot about myself and went a long way in developing my work ethic.

One of the things I noticed was how folks recognized the fact that I had a job and showed more respect than they normally would because of it. I got pulled aside by adults and told to keep doing what I was doing. It became clear they expected more of me than other kids who were apparently just laying around all summer. It was from this energy that I grew confident and learned my place in the world as being one of the "good" ones.

J.G. Robinson

That was over twenty five years ago and the rules haven't changed. You see there's no expiration date on hard work, honor, or integrity. It's not something you grow out of or forget how to do. People still look for all the same qualities and values in the people they meet. This is why it's important we as a people portray these qualities in our workplace and do our best to instill these values in our children.

Respect in the workplace is crucial for many reasons. Often people will define themselves by the positions they hold in society. In the same breath, the absence of a fulfilling career can and often does affect how a person is viewed as well. As a community, we must have enough respect for each other to encourage and support an individual who has either fallen on hard times, or is living an undesirable life that he or she wants to change or improve.

Far too often in our communities we condemn the very ones who were looking to us for support. If we could change this it would help immensely with our professional endeavors, since not many can make it very far in any career without help. When backed with adequate support, a person typically strives harder for success which usually increases their sense of self worth as well as their chance of being successful at their place of employment.

The Answer:

We won't truly be respected amongst ourselves or anyone else in the professional world for that matter until we take control of the sources that create the jobs themselves. We need to own a few more banks in order to grant ourselves better funding, build some of our own hospitals to improve the care of our people. Own a few airlines, and build bigger ships to transport and trade as we would wish internationally.

It would be in our best interest to create more colleges, institutions, and non-profit organizations that could assist in the areas needed to advance our own technology. This way we won't have to rely on everyone else's info and merchandise once we have

The Black Man's Answer

become efficient at developing our own.

DEALING WITH COLORISM

There have been many times when the issue has been raised regarding the shade or complexion of our skin, hair texture, eye color, and other features that may not be considered "the norm" for blacks. The argument over whether fair-skinned blacks progress easier in life over dark-skinned blacks goes back to the slave days between the so called "house" and "field" negro.

However, I have found in my travels and research that this issue is actually bigger than the African American community. I found that dark-skinned individuals of many regions and cultures across the world experience similar treatment in their societies. I have come to believe that this is an issue of beauty more than it is a matter of equality or race.

For whatever reason, it's common for many human beings of all regions to find a lighter complexion and subtle facial features more attractive. Not that there aren't attractive dark-skinned people as well because they definitely exist. It's just that the traits of dark-skinned people are considered overall to be more "common" in most societies. This in itself isn't a bad thing, but typically most people don't want to be labeled as common or ordinary.

We all want to be viewed as being special or unique in our lives. Therefore we tend to crave something special, unique, or different when we choose a mate. As men we naturally want a wife whose beauty outshines all others, and likewise most women would like a mate with traits desirable enough to pass on to their offspring. This would be hard to achieve on both accounts if everyone looked the same.

Basic human genetics tell us that dark-skinned traits are dominant and fair skinned traits are recessive. Therefore, most people understand mating with a dark-skinned person will usually cancel most recessive traits held by the other. Even still from time to time though, one or two of these traits will emerge dominant within us causing a rare find amongst our people.

A certain grade of hair or unusual eye color can be quite stunning to those who have never witnessed a person of color with it. Therefore, all it takes for a dark-skinned individual to draw attention to themselves is to possess an uncommon trait like green eyes for instance, and people of any race will start to take notice.

Meanwhile other blacks bearing witness to this phenomenon may secretly wish to carry the same traits in order to receive the same attention. This can lead to a dissatisfaction of one's own appearance and possible envy of the person with the uncommon trait. In the African American community being "light-skinned" or possessing a lighter complexion is considered by many to be one of these traits.

In my experience, being light-skinned is often viewed by many inside and outside of the race, as the more attractive level of blackness. Therefore, whatever resentment we have within our race between light and dark-skinned African Americans stems from this basic occurrence and is often compounded whenever we feel society has favored one shade of black over another as a determining factor.

This can occur in all aspects of society from a young dark-skinned girl not making the cheerleading squad and noticing a certain light-skinned girl did, to a dark-skinned man getting passed over for a promotion only to see it handed over to a light-skinned co-worker instead.

Now it's important to note that it's debatable as to whether these feelings are even justified to begin with. However, they are out there and exist nonetheless. The fact also remains that no one can control what traits they are born with which leads us to the artificial methods of altering one's appearance. Different types of cosmetics like contacts to change eye color, skin bleaching, hair dying, nose jobs, breast implants, and other cosmetics as well. All tend to serve the same purpose; enhance the outward appearance in order to improve the way we feel about ourselves on the inside. Self esteem to be exact, and as stated before this affects just about everyone.

Evidence of how this plays out on a larger scale can be found in places everywhere like India, the Philippines, Latin America, and other countries as well. All have huge amounts of dark-skinned natural born citizens who are seldom recognized on a public or national level to represent the image of that nation.

Very few of the dark-skinned people in those nations possess great wealth, hold high government positions, or even get chosen to honor their nation in something as simple as a beauty pageant. If you doubt what I say simply look up the most recent winners of beauty pageants from places like, Puerto Rico, Brazil, Colombia, Cuba, or Panama and bear witness for yourself. All of these places have many natural dark-skinned citizens, but you'd have a tough time proving it unless you actually went there.

Whether this is done on purpose or out of blind human nature is debatable. In any case it would appear the dark-skinned inhabitants of many nations have been placed in a lower-class status of most societies. So it should come as no surprise when these same people begin to voice their frustrations against being made to feel inferior.

The Answer:

Despite all that happened to us that got us to this point we have to remember one important thing. **WE ARE ALL THE SAME!** We must not let small differences divide us. It is important we all embrace everyone who identifies as part of the African Diaspora regardless of our complexion. Our brothers and sisters stand strongest together and we must never forget this! Hopefully if addressed properly, we can reduce the amount of misconceptions concerning colorism over time.

J.G. Robinson

ROMANTIC RELATIONSHIPS

In my experience, I've noticed that at the heart of almost every dysfunctional relationship or failed marriage dwells a lack of respect. We must learn not only how to respect each other's ways of doing things, but also how to express ourselves in a reasonable manner when something occurs that displeases us. It's also important to do so without disrespecting or insulting our partners.

This can be a difficult task due to the intense amount of emotions at that time, but it is necessary for the relationship to succeed and withstand the test of time. Shouting and name calling in itself is not a crime we can be arrested for, however depending on the tone and context of what's being said it can still be classified as verbal abuse and nobody wants to be in an abusive relationship.

This is something I've witnessed men and women equally be guilty of in their quest for love. Often these harsh reactions stem from frustration anyway. Let's take the time to make sure our partner feels heard and respected, even when we disagree in what they are saying. Although there's no way to keep the relationship "argument free" completely but it should at least help to diffuse much of the bad energy the other person had pinned up inside of them.

Lastly, in the few incidences where we do slip up and say something we shouldn't have to our loved ones, lets be man or woman enough to apologize and forgive each other for what happened. It is crucial that both sides are able to admit the wrong we were each responsible for. It's too often we make a huge emotional mess in the relationship without properly cleaning it up when it's over. This lack of closure is what causes people to hold grudges about the situation and not let go of the pain they originally felt.

Grudge holding can only bring bad results into the relationship. Let's have enough respect for each other to say "I'm sorry", and work on controlling these issues in the future. If you find your

The Black Man's Answer

partner is unwilling to do this, then you may want to show some respect for yourself and move on without them.

Otherwise there is a high probability that the level of frustration will increase in the relationship as the other person becomes more and more comfortable acting out the bad habits that you keep putting up with. If this is the case, then there's no need to point fingers as you are both guilty for the situation you've created. One partner for being disrespectful, and the other for allowing it to happen over and over again.

The Answer:

According to information published by the *Scholars Strategy Network* in October of 2013, it stated that "back in 1960, 61% of blacks were married, but by 2008 the number had decreased to 32%. It further went on to show blacks also get divorced more often and remarry less frequently than whites." I personally believe this to be a result of the crack epidemic of the eighties, coupled with the prolonged use of government assistance programs such as welfare, cash assistance, child support, EBT cards, Medicaid, and HUD housing.

These circumstances inadvertently discourage marriage and teamwork as they provide outside alternatives for young couples to break up and still manage their lives individually. There are even some people out there who question the necessity for marriage entirely. I myself have heard many ask the question, "Why do we need to get married anyway?"

I have personally found that respect is better shown than taught. It stands out to everyone watching when a man opens a door for a female in public, and likewise it shows when a woman is elegant enough to dress with class to all whom observe her manner. In this day and age so many are quick to judge these views of social manners and etiquette as being sexist or old fashioned. However, these are often the same individuals that will tell you how chivalry is dead.

J.G. Robinson

In many cases, it is difficult to have one without appearing to be the other. The lack of these principles in our society has left many lost, confused, and often contradicting themselves in what they want as a mate. Many men want a sexy wife to take care of home and the kids, while also wanting a woman who's independent with her own income and self reliant. Which sounds great but that leaves one problem fellas, if she can do all that on her own, then what would she need a man for?

Many ladies are often looking for a strong handsome man on the outside, who on the inside is a sensitive, intuitive, compassionate individual who enjoys doing all the things she likes to do together. Alright ladies, are we really looking for a man, or your best female friend in a man's body?

We have to learn how to accept and handle the "differences" found in each other as well as the things we share in common. This is how we find out why our mates need us in their lives to begin with and what our purpose is in the relationship. Once that is established amongst both partners, appreciating each other's strengths and weaknesses becomes easier. This makes respecting each other a much more attainable goal.

FRIENDSHIP

One thing I can personally say about growing up in our culture is that making friends isn't easy. True friendship can be difficult to attain for those of us who are subjected to harsh environments and circumstances. Such conditions tend to breed a lot of distrust between each other. In many cases the art of being friendly has become somewhat rare especially among our young people, making it very difficult to gain and acquire new friends.

The truth is, most of us usually become friends by accident. We may live next door, attend the same classes at school, work together, or go to the same church. This is all fine except the friendship wasn't initiated on purpose, meaning very limited social skills develop when befriending others in this manner.

Trying to make new friends simply because you want to have more can call for a different approach. One that many of us are either too proud to engage in, or simply lack the skills to do so. Far too often I hear my people speak on how easy it is to "cut ties" with someone who may have crossed us. This is fine when dealing with strangers, however this same method should not be used on those we need and love.

Unfortunately, there are some of us who do practice this method with our loved ones only to receive horrible results. These kinds of tactics often result in isolation and depression once we are left bitter and lonely. Tools like forgiveness and reconciliation must be used to maintain and support our friends as well. Let's be careful not to exhibit poor inadequate behavior within the relationship or it will slowly but surely deteriorate the friendship altogether.

The Answer:

Many don't realize that whether we are in a relationship with our friends, family, or coworkers. All humans need to be treated in a certain manner. We all need to be shown dignity, respect, and consideration. The truth is that once we figure it out for one of us, the formula is usually the same for everyone else. We just have to be willing to keep trying especially with the ones we really need in our lives.

Chapter 4
Economics

THE ART OF EARNING MONEY

There are so many different ways an individual can make money in America. If a person possesses a good work ethic, a vision, and a sense of creativity, almost anything is possible. It's disheartening to see so many young African Americans resort to illegal activities just to survive. The activities I'm speaking of range from drugs, guns, tax schemes, identity theft, prostitution, and even armed robbery.

If only more of us understood that entrepreneurship runs in our blood, we just have to do a better job of pursuing our dreams within the accepted ways of our society. Money can be made in our own back yards if we are simply clever enough to "legally" tap into it.

Wherever there are large groups of people there stands the potential to make a dollar, and the black community is no exception. This is the reason why we have so many outside entities operating businesses within our neighborhoods. Remember this the next time you shop at a convenient store owned by a person of Middle Eastern descent. Or when we go to the local beauty supply store and buy products from a person of Asian descent.

We should ask ourselves why are we supporting these people's businesses when many of them won't even hire us. They rarely give back to our communities and usually don't live in the same area they run their businesses in. You won't see them attending church beside you on Sunday morning, and I doubt you'd be able to find them at your children's school on Parent/Teacher night. They have no allegiance or loyalty towards our people whatsoever and its time we learn to disconnect from them and realize the money they are making off of us should be coming back to us!

The Black Man's Answer

There's a reason why many of them have moved half way around the world just to sell hair products and cigarettes to us in our communities. If they could've gotten rich in their own lands I'm sure they would have done so, but they couldn't so they came to us. Meanwhile many of our people struggle to make a minimum wage salary only to turn around and give it to these other cultures for their often over-priced products. This has to stop.

The stores located in our community should belong to us, ran by us, and have the potential to hire more of us. Any business not of our people should at least network with other black owned businesses or organizations to provide opportunities for the local African Americans of that area to prosper.

For instance, if a foreign owned business wants to open in our community then we need to ensure at least a few blacks are guaranteed spots on the payroll. Furthermore, we should insist a minimum requirement of annual donations be made to our local churches and charities as a statement they are in support of our community.

If not, then a boycott of all businesses who do not comply is in order and they can go make money elsewhere off some other culture. You see when it comes to money and power it's not just one culture we have to look out for, because they are all in it to win it.

Once we have gained control of our communities in this fashion it will be much easier for us to go into business for ourselves and provide jobs to each other. This will ensure money circulates in our own areas which over time should improve the impoverished conditions that exist in low income areas for our people.

The next part of the puzzle is that we take the time to establish our own and have the good sense to support each other when we do it. If successful, the day will come where we won't need to seek employment outside of our communities because the jobs produced for each other and by each other will be plentiful.

Finally, is the overall lack of knowledge that keeps many of us in the poor state we are in. Let's be sure we have exhausted all avenues of possible employment before we give up and resort to illegal activity. There are many instances where job positions are posted in forums that most of us are simply unaware of. There are so many times I've heard young blacks say, "I didn't know that was an option", when asked why they didn't make different choices in their past that would have benefitted them in their future.

There is no real way to point out every opportunity that could be available to a person in every location, therefore it's up to everyone to be relentless in their search for the ideal position that fits them. It's important to remember we don't always have to strive to be a Doctor or a Lawyer.

A good percentage of African Americans have no interest in such careers anyway. It's more advantageous for us to look for good careers that may have been overlooked and could provide the same wealth and security we desire. Opportunities can range, from anything to being a locksmith, jeweler, state park ranger, or even joining the Peace Corps.

There are many great respectable jobs that don't require the intimidating "overpriced" college career path that many of us can't afford or simply don't want to do. In all honesty, even something as simple as pushing a hot dog cart could earn over $30,000.00 a year if done in the right locations. At the end of the day, most of us are only limited by our own imagination and willingness to work.

The Answer:

The State of working America published that "in 2010 African Americans had the highest poverty rate at 27.4 percent, followed by Hispanics at 26.6 percent and whites at 9.9 percent." Today we have more millionaires and billionaires walking amongst us than ever before, but it seems these individuals are few and far between. They often act independently from each other in their humanitarian efforts or choose to ignore the poverty situation altogether and end up benefiting only themselves.

A system, method, or organization must be established by us that ensures the circulation of wealth and resources throughout our communities. This will allow those seeking change to pool their resources and combine efforts to improve our communities here and abroad. This way we get taken seriously when we speak about the funding our communities need.

Like better schools, roads, transportation, parks, libraries, jobs, land, and so on. All these services could be provided or negotiated by us through this system or newfound organization we have established. As stated before it simply depends on how much we want it.

SAVING MONEY

I think it's a fair statement to say that most of us are aware we should save some money whenever we can to get through hard times as they arise. For many of us saving money is hard to do when we're barely able to make it from paycheck to paycheck. However, when we finally do get some of that money we've so desperately needed, it is imperative that some remain tucked away for future use.

Things happen in life, and when they do we must have something to fall back on. So, in order to make it through these tough periods we have to look for creative ways outside of our normal job income to make additional money or purchase things that will increase in value overtime.

This is what the financial world calls "acquiring assets" and it plays a direct role in establishing the "Net Worth" of our households. Otherwise we may end up burdening our family members or friends with our hardships by constantly relying on them for money.

The most simple and easiest way to save money is through discipline and moderation. This is something we all can achieve by exercising a little restraint. We don't have to have everything we see, even though we may really want it. It's important we learn to plan and wait. I believe anything worth having today will still be valuable tomorrow. Let's not allow our feelings or the peer pressure of advertising and salesmanship get the better of us and fall victim to impulsive shopping.

If you're only making $1500.00 a month it's probably not a good idea to buy a brand-new vehicle that will cost over $600.00 a month, especially if you're already paying $900.00 a month for an apartment. This clearly doesn't add up when you include the additional monthly costs you'll have for utilities, gas, car insurance, groceries, phone services, and other personal needs. Not to mention the scenario mentioned above is based on individuals who are single. One can only imagine what it must be like for those who have to support children as well, which is often the case in many of our situations.

It's also worth mentioning that the jobs many of us hold today may not necessarily be around for us when tomorrow comes. Work hours routinely get cut and people get laid off all the time, so what little money we do make is often not even dependable. This makes long term purchases such as auto loans and thirty-year mortgage contracts a complete gamble to us. Especially since most of us are unsure if we will even be employed for the next six months, let alone for thirty years consecutively!

Trying to balance the lives of several in a household off such little income and job security is a precarious position for anyone to endure. It's no wonder why there are those of us who end up relying on welfare and other government assistance programs to survive. These circumstances make for a hard life and unfortunately this way of living is all too common in our communities. This often ends up being an impossible formula to progress with, but a perfect formula for poverty and struggle.

The problem is these days too many of us are concerned about "looking the part" and trying to have the same things everyone else has. How can we own the same cars, electronics, clothes, cell phones, jewelry, or hairdos, as everyone else when most of us only possess a fraction of their wealth?

Nevertheless, there are those of us out there without jobs who make sure to wear all the latest fashions. There are also those of us who need medical attention for ailments such as an ongoing cough, chronic back pain, or overdue dental work who can't seem to afford it. Yet somehow these same individuals will often have a large screen television in their home, complete with cable, a shelf full of movies, and the latest video games for their kids.

It's important we do a good job of prioritizing our finances. Failure to do so means we will never reach a stable foundation where all of our basic needs are met. This causes many of us to be consistently unable to save and if we can't save then we can never build ourselves financially. This issue leaves us with no choice but to use loans and credit cards to make ends meet effectively making many of victims of the debt system.

When it comes to business matters we are frequently dealing with high interest rates and laws that condone the taxation of our income. This means we often end up paying back creditors and struggling to maintain a credit score that can fluctuate according to whatever the controlling authorities deem necessary.

The consequences should we fail at this are financial pitfalls such as repossession of our vehicles, foreclosures of our homes, and for some even bankruptcy. If this pattern continues, many of us would never be able to build, grow, own, or make any kind of progress in this capitalistic American society.

There are many who already speculate that the future of the "middle class" here in America will be decreasing as the gap between the poor and the wealthy increases. This dilemma, if left unchecked has the potential to permanently sentence many blacks to generation upon generation of poverty. Ultimately leaving us with no choice but to live in a lower class of society under the mercy of those who have successfully manipulated the system. This is not a conclusion I care to see, but it can very much become a reality if we don't unite our efforts and help each other through this.

J.G. Robinson

There are many within our communities who have become quite savvy with economic planning and strategy. Unfortunately, not enough to change the vast gap in wealth between our people and the rest of America. We need more of us to become aware and "active" with building and improving our economy.

This way those of us who possess the capability for economic growth can practice it for the rest of us. This should allow those who aren't in a position to contribute on a huge scale such as myself can follow their lead and provide the support needed in the streets and communities.

The Answer:

The remedy to this dilemma can be summed up in one word, "Sacrifice!" There should be a simple order of responsibility that must be met before indulging in flamboyant, overpriced luxuries. At the end of the day we are only making others rich by purchasing their merchandise anyway. Necessary items such as food, clothes, shelter, healthcare, and affordable transportation should always be taken care of before buying anything else.

Furthermore, there are other adjustments that can be made on our end. We can split the cost of that apartment and utilities mentioned earlier by finding a decent roommate to pay the other half. We can reduce the amount of that car by settling for an older used model, or possibly eliminate the cost altogether by carpooling with someone we know and helping them out with gas money and repairs once in a while.

We can also take the time to get a bus pass or ride the subway if we reside in an area that has one, until we save up enough cash to do more. With expenses such as groceries we can make it a point to eat out less, and look for sales and bargains around town in the local supermarkets. It's also not a bad idea to use a coupon whenever possible to get the price down off items such as toilet paper, diapers, or hygiene products. This is important since many of these items are more of a "need" than a "want". Just these few suggestions alone can save us hundreds of dollars a month if used correctly.

There are many other ways possible to reduce spending and make the money we earn go further. Like most things in life it is solely up to the creativity and dedication of the person making the money to see how far they can maximize their cash flow. Once we have mastered reducing our expenses and saving the excess money, we can then move on to learning what to do with the new savings we have now accumulated. We must remember the importance of this because it's no one else's fault but our own if we aren't living the way we need to establish happiness in this world.

INVESTING

It's not enough to just earn and save our money. We must also know how to use it once we've acquired it in order to make progress and gain wealth. The concept of making sound investments for ourselves must become a reality.

We should look for positive ways to use our money in a manner that works for us and will pay off in the long run. Unfortunately, it's hard to make progress until we have established a basic foundation for survival. This should be mastered first before attempting growth on a higher level.

The first phase is establishing a foundation for everyday survival and can be summed up in five categories I like to refer to as the **"Five Fingers of Survival"**.

These five categories are as follows:

1. Food
2. Clothing
3. Shelter
4. Healthcare
5. Transportation

These are the items needed for all to sustain a basic existence and survive in our society. Most are well aware that we need food, clothing, shelter, and good health. It's also important to remember all humans need a certain amount of mobility as well. This is true whether it be a child on their way to school in the morning, or an elderly person who needs to get to a doctor's appointment.

Reliable transportation is often overlooked by many but just as important to achieve a secure foundation to grow from. Acquiring these items is of course the first step. The next step is setting up a system for ourselves that makes sure we continue to have them on a consistent basis.

The Black Man's Answer

As we all know food runs out, clothes get old, rent is always due, people get sick, and cars break down. When these things happen we need a system that will allow us to overcome these hardships without jeopardizing our entire lifestyle. Establishing such a system is the first crucial blow in defeating the cycle of poverty.

Once we have achieved stability in our lives and have begun to possess a little extra money and resources, we can then focus on the next phase which is what I like to refer to as the "**Five Fingers of Progress**".

These five categories are as follows:

6. Education/Knowledge
7. Networking (who you know)
8. Establish Savings
9. Eliminating Debt
10. Acquiring assets

With these concepts successfully mastered we can gradually build and advance ourselves into a better state of living. Using education and increased knowledge we can gain the tools needed to seek better paying jobs, or become self-employed and even provide jobs to others. This allows for improved networking amongst other worthy individuals with valuable skills.

This also allows us to pursue and build things for our community much easier and faster than we could if we tried it as individuals. If we eliminate the debt we owe by paying loans off early, getting better interest rates, or finding cheaper alternatives of what we want altogether. This would free up extra income for things we've always wanted to do and help with improving our credit scores.

With this being achieved we should have no trouble setting up savings for our children for things such as trust funds and college plans. It's also worth mentioning to keep an ever-watchful eye out for local auctions of needed items such as cars, foreclosed homes, land, and any other assets that may come in handy. This along with staying mindful and aware of all possible tax breaks and benefits, so we can and make the system work for us.

Last but definitely not least is the concept of acquiring assets. This represents the stocks, bonds, real estates, small owned businesses, and everything else financial advisors, and stock brokers speak of when mentioning investing. The bottom line is, if it will make or save you money after purchasing it, then go for it. If not, then think carefully before purchasing it because chances are you are only making others rich.

I refer to these two concepts as the "**Five Fingers**" because when all five fingers are united they form together to make a mighty fist, which is what we in our community need to fight for our survival. However, there are those of us out there who are trying to fight for survival without even forming the first fist yet. This is an obvious reason why many of us keep losing in the fight for wealth and stability.

Think about it, how many fights would you win if you had one bad hand and the other was tied behind your back? Well believe it or not there are many of us out there who are trying to make it work with barely four of the ten items I've mentioned. This typically results in an unstable life of financial barriers and disappointments.

We in the black community need to educate ourselves on what to do with our income, and have the courage to risk losing what little we have in order to gain more. It's also worth saying that after we master our own financial positions we should combine strength with others who have done the same. This is critical because we stand strongest together, and there is little chance we will lose any fights, when we join with others who seek the same security in life as we do.

The Answer:

According to information published in <u>USA Today</u> "in 2007, prior to the recession, there were 41 banks with majority African

The Black Man's Answer

American ownership. There were 44 banks in 1986, the year Congress passed a law designating February as National Black History Month. Today, the number of black-owned banks has fallen to just 23 institutions."

Investing on some level must be done by us all. If you can't do it alone then find a partner. If both of you can't do it together than find group. No matter how it gets done we must acquire stocks, bonds, land, real estate, small businesses and everything else that separates the haves from the have not's in this world. This is not an option. In order to achieve any real progress, we simply have to make it happen!

MASTERING CREDIT

Learning how to manage credit is a game we all have to play. It tells financial institutions whether or not we are worthy of granting and repaying loans. So just like with any other game we have to know the rules in order to perform well. Credit and money management in general has to be taught and practiced in the home in order to prevent or reduce the amount of mistakes made by us out in society.

We must teach what a credit score is and explain the importance of maintaining a good one. Many people I've met in my travels not only don't understand it, but really have no clue about how to improve it. It should become a common goal for us in our communities to practice methods of managing and reducing debt in every aspect of our lives.

It should also be viewed as a personal failure on our part if our kids don't hear about these things until it's time to make a major purchase. In which case they often get told they have no credit, or even bad credit depending on how financially irresponsible their parents may have been. It's not uncommon to hear stories of kids who already have debt listed under their name and social security number at a young age by their guardians.

Such neglect by us in teaching the proper financial fundamentals can leave our children in the sad position of having to take whatever deal they can get. Doing business this way routinely comes with whatever lousy rates the sales representative will offer. This lack of knowledge often leaves us completely at the mercy of the seller and any unscrupulous business practices they can dream up. This is not a position any consumer should want to be in.

We should be preparing ourselves and our children to go out into this capitalistic society to succeed. Let's make sure we establish a good line of credit early for our kids by opening and maintaining bank accounts or trust funds in their name for them. We should also teach them how to write checks, use debit cards, and comprehend interest rates, so they don't get taken advantage of by those who already know the game.

The Answer:

We must always remember to educate ourselves and each other on what it takes to attain a better lifestyle financially. There are so many ways to achieve wealth and prosperity. There is no one simple formula we all can rely on to get there. One suggestion would be for us to get together and come up with a program to teach and mentor our youth specifically on circumstances with money.

History tells us that the current credit system or "FICO score" was not in place until 1989. So this is not a game in which we have had a lot of time to master. This means many of our elders aren't able to provide guidance on a system they never took part in back when they established themselves financially. So we have to do our part in breaking this down for ourselves.

BUILDING AN INHERITANCE

When people die in our communities, it's too often we leave our loved ones behind with nothing but heartache and bills to be paid. This often results in additional stress because now our relatives must find a way to make ends meet while paying the funeral costs associated with the deceased and possibly having to manage a separate estate as well.

Issues such as selling a home or deciding the fate of any children who may have been orphaned as a result of this tragedy can be mentally and emotionally draining. In many cases the state is left to take over the matter which is rarely beneficial to any of the parties involved.

As a community we simply cannot accept this. We can't expect to get ahead as a people if we allow our children to start over at zero or in some cases below zero because they took on our unpaid debt and started out in the negative. The children are our future and they must be set up to succeed in a world we know they won't understand.

Help and guidance on how to navigate financial mishaps is vital! Efforts must be made to set aside trust funds, college plans, and adequate insurance for their future. We should also focus on acquiring certain assets such as "paid-off" property, real estate, or a profitable business so they can survive in the same manner we did or better before their time is up on this earth.

There's no reason why we can't apply at least one or two of these concepts during our lifespan to assist our children with. To do anything less should be regarded as a parenting failure. Only extreme conditions such as untimely deaths, incapacitation, or mental breakdowns should serve as reasonable circumstances for our children being left to figure it out on their own. To the rest of us who are fully capable physically, mentally, and spiritually, there really is no excuse. We absolutely "**MUST**" establish a decent inheritance for our youth!

The Answer:

According to data published by the *United States Census Bureau*, "African Americans still consistently wield the lowest Net Worth amongst all other groups here in America." An effort must be made to ensure our community maintains reasonable securities for the assets earned during our lives.

Goals such as acquiring affordable life insurance, maintaining updated wills, establishing executors of our estates, paying in advance for our own funeral arrangements, and establishing trust funds have to become a priority.

In many cases any one of these things being done in advance could make a significant difference in our children's lives. We must ensure that we have left something for them before transitioning from this world. Seriously, what's the point of spending a lifetime working if we can't achieve that one simple thing?

Chapter 5
Perceptions

TRUST IN OUR MEN

In many ways black males have been demonized in our society. It's rarely admitted by others, but we are often viewed by many as having a higher tendency to break the laws rather than abide by them. This is often the unspoken reason why very few question why we are incarcerated at such a higher rate than other cultures. It's almost as if we were somehow built with less morals than most, or a lower level of decency.

It seems the underlying theme for many is that a black man is the first to participate in theft, engage in drug use, or commit violent crimes in our society. The reverse meaning of that stigma is we are also viewed as the last to selflessly volunteer for a cause, increase another's wealth, or save the lives of the people around us. Interestingly enough, this notion does not come exclusively from outside of our culture either. There are a significant number of blacks who accept and perpetuate these beliefs as well.

For instance, I personally have heard many stories from unhappy black women. Many of them were so fixated on portraying themselves as the victims of failed relationships, and marriages, that I'm not sure if they really comprehended or cared, just how much damage they were doing to the image of the black male to achieve this!

I love and always will love our beautiful black women, but honestly when I heard black males being referred to by words such as a deadbeat, liar, or cheater it was coming from them most of the time. Now obviously there are some guys out there who deserve those titles, not everyone out there is a respectable person. However, I cannot condone the endless bashing and insulting of them no more

J.G. Robinson

than I could condone a woman being repeatedly referred to as a whore, slut, or gold-digger even if she does participate in prostitution, had a history of being promiscuous, or is very materialistic.

Trust me when I tell you nothing good will come from condemning each other, and if it did we would have resolved the issues amongst us already by now. We've got to stop wasting emotion and energy on things that don't help any of us, and instead focus on the productive goals we can accomplish together.

The black man has had his fair share of unfavorable views and stereotypes from all sides. In fact, from my experience there are many from other cultures who still dread the idea of their sweet innocent daughter bringing home a dark-skinned negro to add to the family tree.

In some cases, we may even have experienced some difficulty befriending each other. Sometimes this happens due to being from a different class of wealth, or being of a different culture of blackness altogether. Many issues can arise from feeling distant amongst your own people. Folks tend to respond in a variety of ways when made to feel out of place as if they do not belong.

People often develop hurt feelings, misconceptions about each other, and depending on the degree of the misunderstanding sometimes even violence can occur. Therefore, it's not uncommon for some of our young to seek out others in order to find acceptance and protection against those who may have ill intentions towards them.

As the group grows stronger and larger the competition grows and at some point, it becomes necessary to see who has the bigger and better group of brothers. When this happens the contest to find out who the best is begins. We refer to these groups as being "gangs", and most of us in America are familiar with the issues that gangs can bring.

These issues often contribute to what mainstream media likes to refer to as "black on black" crime. I myself don't subscribe to that notion, I believe a crime is a crime despite the skin tone of the individual. I will agree however, that unity and coexisting together is something we could stand to do a little better on.

For instance, if there are instances where American blacks don't like Haitian blacks, and blacks from African nations don't identify with South American blacks, while blacks in England think themselves better than Jamaican blacks, then how can we ever hope to progress as a people? If we allow ourselves to interact in this way, then our resources and ambitions will remain separated and weak as opposed to united and strong.

Black people from all over the world in Mississippi, Trinidad, Brazil, India, Ethiopia, or Australia, must learn to see and accept each other as brethren. It is important we eradicate what's really at the heart of this matter which is distrust. A different language, culture, religion, income, or social class is not a reason to forsake our distant brethren.

It is vital we work together to help restore the lost trust that should be amongst each other in our community and abroad internationally. This way we can rebuild the strong positive image we should have in our culture and become the trusted son's, brothers, uncles, husband's, father's and ultimately the responsible citizens we know we are capable of being.

The Answer:

To help improve this situation I recommend we reach out to each other and establish a reliable network amongst ourselves to help with each other's issues. We should be capable of providing knowledge and even employment to those who need it in order to improve the quality of our lives.

It is important for us to have individuals who are willing to dedicate themselves to the cause. This should go a long way in helping to reestablish the bonds of trust needed amongst each other. Only then will we see a positive long-lasting change in how the

J.G. Robinson

black male is viewed in our society.

TRUST IN OUR WOMEN

As our counterparts, black women here in America have also inherited a less than admirable reputation from society. They are often depicted as being emotional, overly dramatic, and ill tempered, by popular culture. It's important to remember our sisters have had to fight to establish a dignified position in this society.

This coupled with having a slavery based history of not always being able to depend on their fellow black males for support and protection, have caused some women to resort to unsavory methods to survive and make a place for themselves and their children in this world.

I feel our women are routinely exploited by many men "including our own" for sexual conquests rather than companionship, marriage, or simple friendship. Therefore, it's no wonder after years of constantly having to do it alone and on their own, that some of them may have resorted to the crude behavior witnessed regularly in many low-income communities.

I attribute most of this as the primary cause to issues such as prostitution, drugs, poverty, and their toleration of domestic violence. Unfortunately, these circumstances have taught some of these women that they need to do whatever it takes to survive even if it means sacrificing their dignity to dance naked in a strip club, have sex for a few dollars, publish a "sex tape" for cheap fame, or simply getting pregnant to collect government assistance and child support.

You see we must remember that our woman's role was crucial in helping us survive slavery and still persists in the poverty stricken areas of America today. She had no choice but to endure the hardships of those times and struggle to keep it together for her own sanity and way of life. We must also remember that she did so regardless of anyone's approval or judgment over her actions. It is this very grit and tenacity that still resonates within the spirits of many of them today. Our women have proven they will make it one way or another, with or without anyone's help.

There is however a reoccurring theme here which is simply that our sisters need help and adequate support. It's hard to make it in life alone even for a few years, let alone their whole life and usually with kids. As a black man, I see it as our primary responsibility to assist our sisters in all aspects of life, and that goes for all of them not just the ones we love. We should extend a helping hand to those we work with, live next to, go to church with, attend class with and so on.

If we see our black women walking we should never ride past them without offering a ride. I feel a black woman should never starve if there is a black man near that can assist her. Once we truly learn to embrace and support our black women as we should, I believe many of those jezebel-like ways that some have adopted will begin to dissipate. That tough exterior some of them carry will also fade and the true gentle loving grace and kindness of our beautiful sisters will shine once again for all to see.

However, for many it will take time for them to let their guard down and allow this to happen. In any case for those of us who aren't in their situation we have to understand living such a life in many ways is like fighting a war, and we shouldn't expect them to put down their swords and take off their armor while they are still on the battlefield. I do believe however, if we support them, their image will improve, and the culture will blossom together as a whole.

The Answer:

First, to those who are in this situation and are able to, we need to make sure we get off any government assisted programs if we are able to make the change. These services should be seen as temporary just to help people who are going through hard times get back on their feet. They should never be used as a free ride through life. It's even worse if it's done from generation to generation which is totally unacceptable.

J.G. Robinson

It's important to know the welfare program was invented in **1935** by President Franklin D. Roosevelt. Food stamps (EBT card) were created in **1964** by President Lyndon B. Johnson, and child support was established in **1975** by Congress under President Gerald Ford.

Now if we were to measure this time in comparison to how long our women have been making due in this world before the creation of these programs, we would see how these are all fairly new systems that have been presented to our people. The truth is black women were more than capable of taking care of themselves, their children, and even their men if needed, long before all of this so-called government assistance was invented. So, there's no point in acting as if we can't live without using them today.

Our women have already proven they can deal with the worst life has to offer during the slave era here in America, and even still today in other countries where many of these programs don't exist. This is why it's important we don't subscribe to the idea that we can't make it without this stuff because we know for a fact we can.

Unfortunately, there are many (including ourselves) who have forgotten this fact. The sooner we stop allowing them to feed us, and get back to feeding ourselves will we once again be privileged to see the full respect, and dignity owed return to our people.

TRUST IN OUR YOUTH

In my experience it's not uncommon for us to scoff at our youth when they bring up ideas or goals that are different than our own. Usually we end up discrediting these thoughts because of their obvious lack of experience, or because they simply don't have the understanding or resources needed to take on the task. It is important for us to realize these are exactly the kind of things we need to encourage and support our children with.

It takes a young fresh mind and spirit to forge paths not yet walked by others. So who better to lead us than our very own flesh and blood? Sure, some of them may be impatient, selfish, and even careless, but that's why we parents are there to guide them and reduce the pitfalls that lay before them.

Once they realize you "truly" believe in them, don't worry, they will listen. In many cases I've witnessed, most of our kids would rather die than disappoint or let down parents who have consistently loved, supported, and listened to them all their lives.

So, if your daughter smiles and says she's going to be a scuba diver for a living, even though you may currently live in poverty out in a location that's nowhere near an ocean, think hard before you respond. If properly nurtured, her dreams may take her (and you) further than you could've imagined.

The Answer:

We must invest in our children! I don't mean solely by sending them to high priced colleges or private schools, but by instilling love, encouragement, and other positive emotions into their very souls. For most low income blacks the success of our kids come from individuals outside of the home. Like that teacher who wouldn't give up on them, that football coach who saw something more in them, or that preacher who told them to hold on for a better day.

It's fine to get support from others, but we have to understand no one has a stronger emotional pull on our kids than we do as their parents. We must learn to harness this influential ability and use it to properly craft our children into the fantastic individuals we all know they can be.

COPING WITH SOCIETY

Over the years I have seen how most issues that receive notoriety in the community are the ones that get the attention of the masses. In other words, it's not really important unless it's on the radio or television. One thing I feel that would help is if we depended less on what popular opinion was concerning us as a whole. Don't get me wrong, it is always wise to know how we are perceived by others, however it can be a deterrent if not utilized properly.

For instance, if a young black male, let's call him "Dante" was naturally tall and fast, the popular opinion of what his stature should be used for is typically to play basketball. For him not to do so is usually regarded as a waste of talent and ability by those around him. This is because in many low-income urban areas this would be seen as his ticket to a better life. So much so that he would never be taken seriously anytime he suggested trying other talents, activities, or potential interests.

Needless to say, Dante eventually conforms to the opinion of friends and family in order to receive their much-needed respect and approval. The downside is that in most cases pursuing one talent usually squashes any dreams or desires he may have had otherwise. Especially since the level of commitment and dedication required to do well in such a competitive field, doesn't leave much free time for anything else.

This means that any other aspirations Dante may have had will be left unrecognized. Dreams such as space travel, sailing ships, snowboarding, politics, or even becoming a race car driver. Many of which would have been impressive feats for a brother in Dante's position and a milestone achievement for his family, and our culture.

Instead by following the popular opinion of those around him he'll more than likely choose to play basketball, possibly play well in high school, and if lucky even get a scholarship to college. This would be a good thing except most choose an easy major which will

The Black Man's Answer

most likely result in a college degree that he has no interest in. This type of decision-making places all of Dante's hopes of success on an over-saturated market of tall black guys trying to make it into the NBA.

Unfortunately, the chances of him actually reaching this goal are about as slim as winning the lottery. Think about it, would you encourage your child to buy lottery tickets for a living until he or she wins? Because the odds aren't much better when it comes to aspirations of being a famous athlete, musician, or entertainer.

Many of our young men end up getting thrown into a huge category of folks who were told the same things and fed the same lines Dante was years ago by his friends and family. Some for football, some for Rap music, others for track and field, but the pigeonhole effect remains the same these young folk. Many of whom will more than likely suffer the same or worse fate than Dante did.

We can't all do the same thing black America, nor should we try to! We are incredibly diverse and have many talents and attributes worthy of expanding and capitalizing on. Instead of placing so much emphasis on physical ability, what someone should have helped Dante to understand is how to develop his mind and seek out his passions.

This is by far the most powerful tool anyone can have if they want to succeed. Our American society will always spend more time critiquing what "**has happened**" rather than promoting what "**should be happening**", especially when it comes to black communities. Therefore, it cannot be stressed enough how important it is for us to support and nurture those who dare to walk a different path of blackness.

The Answer:

According to data published by _Black Demographics_, "the most popular professions chosen by blacks were in healthcare, education, and social assistance." It is important for us to become more encouraging of others who don't fit the "traditional mold". As I've said before, we can't all do the same things. Therefore, we shouldn't have to face judgment from our own should we ever decide to step outside the stereotypical box a little.

RELATIONSHIPS WITH OTHERS

How many times have we lived or worked right next to someone who may have been able to help us in our situation yet remained quiet because they were of another culture, race, or just seemed weird to us? I personally can recall my relatives saying things like, "we are out of flour, well I would ask the neighbors next door but I don't know about those people, so I guess we'll just have to make due with what we have".

Afterwards the statement was usually backed up by additional comments regarding how different their culture was, or how they may have had different standards of cleanliness, which prompted us not to trust their preparation of food or something along those lines. Meanwhile we were going out of our way to buy something we probably could've gotten for free from our fellow neighbors down the street. As an eight year old boy I remember thinking, "I'm sure they got it from the store just like we did so what's the big deal?" However, I would never have said such a thing aloud to my elders.

The truth is we've all said or thought similar things about someone at some point in our lives. The problem lies however in the details. First of all, if we live next to someone we should at least take the time to get to know them and maybe even invite them over for dinner sometime. It's called being neighborly, polite, and plain old friendly. This is something I've rarely seen my people offer to those we don't know, especially in our low-income communities, or when dealing with those of a different culture, race, or religion.

Furthermore, the fact that I heard this kind of talk as little boy is also indicative of another issue. We must be careful what we say around our youth, as it sticks to their young impressionable minds (as you can see I'm now a grown man who can still recall what was said). Statements like this may seem harmless and common in our households, but they ultimately breed distrust and give birth to ignorant stereotypes regarding people and cultures we don't know or understand.

So as the little boy grew, what do you think my response was as a full-grown man who was looking to buy a home that happened to be located next to neighbors of a different culture than myself? You got it! I leaned over to my wife and said, "it's not a bad deal but I don't know about living next to those people, I guess we'll just have to keep looking". Now I wonder where I got that way of thinking from?!

The Answer:

It's to our advantage to branch out and learn more about others and how they go about surviving in this world. Many valuable skills can be learned and applied from others to make our own lives better, as long as we are not too proud or arrogant to admit it. It's also harder for an enemy to stand against us when they can't be sure of the others in the community with whom we may have networked or be affiliated with.

Also, as a rule of thumb we must remember, **"If they can't talk with you, then they are going to talk about you."** Which is always a bad thing because a person who talks about you without knowing you is only capable of providing incomplete, or incorrect information concerning you. So, since we can't stop another person from talking altogether, it serves as a benefit to us to let them in and give them the real story of who we are on our terms.

J.G. Robinson

PRACTICING FORGIVENESS

What can be said about forgiveness that hasn't already been said? From the legendary Jesus Christ to the Honorable Reverend Dr. Martin Luther King Jr., forgiveness has been drilled into us as the primary weapon against handling the ills of society. Yet somehow...we still don't get it. In many cases, those of us who do understand, don't practice it unless we have no other option or feel we can receive some direct benefit from it in return.

Most of us seek revenge every time someone hurts us whether it was intentional or not. Those who may not be capable of exacting revenge for themselves, often end up hiding the pain away from everyone keeping it bottled up and pretending it never happened. Tragically carrying the weight of the trauma around like a bad cold, spreading infectious energy called distrust through grudges and resentment from one person to another.

Unfortunately, many of us end up contracting and passing this energy around in our relationships. It can taint the bonds held with our significant others, children, friends, coworkers or anyone who dares to get close enough to demand a sincere relationship from us. It's sad to say, but these are the loved ones who will have to uncover the ugly truths that have been hiding within our spirit. However, when these vulnerabilities are finally exposed, may God help them with what's to come next. This is because we will often lash out or attack anyone we have to, in order to maintain our pride, dignity, and sense of respect.

We will do everything in our power to keep them from making us feel as weak, vulnerable, helpless, or ashamed as that evil person made us feel on that day so long ago. In fact, some of us may have even made a promise to ourselves that no one would **EVER** make us feel as low as we felt back then. This way we would never have to endure the low level of self-esteem, self-worth, or self-value we felt when we were placed in that position the first time.

The Black Man's Answer

It's a vow like no other and becomes a pretty detailed and elaborate plan to build a strong, impenetrable, mental and spiritual fortress within ourselves. This is a plan that may even have succeeded except for one vital flaw; **all human beings need each other**. The phrase "no man is an island unto himself" has truth to it.

Human beings are pack animals who need each other to survive. Mankind is not meant to run off like hermits into the hills and spend eternity as separate individuals without interacting with each other. Therefore, it does no good to build a mighty emotional fortress within ourselves, if we constantly have to keep letting people in it.

These are always new people, strange people, sometimes by blood, sometimes by law, some we want, others not so much, but in every case, they bring all of their flaws with them for us to deal with. Now we could all drive ourselves crazy trying to decide who should be allowed to get close to us and who shouldn't. When all we really need to learn to learn is how to truly forgive and move on.

It's time we forgave those who wronged us. We must also forgive ourselves for allowing them to do those things to us in the first place. These emotions are quite normal as it is simply human nature to feel this way when someone takes advantage of us. What's not normal is developing long lasting habits concerning how we treat others who had nothing to do with the original incident. As mature adults we all should strive to develop tools to cope with and handle these situations that produce this toxic energy. This should free us from these destructive cycles we get caught up in.

Those who don't learn these skills often become statistics in our culture. Issues of divorce, broken homes, drugs, alcohol, violence, depression, and suicide are often the sad side effects for people who don't know the value of forgiveness. It should come as no surprise that our community has more than its fair share of people suffering from these ailments.

It is my belief that if we properly taught each other what the consequences of "not forgiving" were, then more of us would get better at moving passed any unfortunate events we may have

J.G. Robinson

experienced. Most of us aren't even aware that the reason we are struggling is because we refuse to forgive. Many of us are still holding a grudge and blaming the ones who wronged us to begin with. At some point we have to realize that doing this hasn't helped or changed our lives one bit. Even if we continued to blame them for twenty more years it still would not help the situation. Therefore, a wise person must realize there is no other choice but to simply **let it go**, so they can move on and flourish in the rest of their life.

Sad to say, not much has changed in this aspect. These days some have confused the term forgive with forget. Phrases such as "**I can forgive but I'll never forget**", can often mislead people on what forgiveness truly is. This can cause a person to mistake or use one in place of another which will only cause confusion and frustration when applied improperly. There are no shortcuts with this, we must do it right.

It's important for us to realize forgiveness is a gift that we give to ourselves first and foremost. It's the only way to stop the pain, let go, and move forward with our lives. When we've mastered how to do this, then we can learn to forgive those who wronged us as well. Once, this has been achieved and we've gotten the hang of it. The best moves we could make is to teach those we know and love how to do the same. This is the only way to keep our relationships fruitful and our spirits positive and bright as they should be.

In these times it's typical that everyone feels entitled to the things they want in life. We often feel like we should be receiving better treatment from our parents, our lovers, our siblings, our kids, our teachers, our co-workers, and even our government. Everyone we know is held accountable for the things we want and need in life and we are quick to complain or criticize when the situation doesn't meet our expectations.

The thing is however, that when the roles are reversed and it's our turn to please others, it's important to know that we often fall short in their eyes as well. We either didn't do it right, fast enough, or for the right reasons. Therefore just about everyone goes through life feeling as if their needs are never really met by others.

You see patience, tolerance, acceptance, and understanding for everyone is the answer. However, it's not enough just to know the answer to a dilemma, it has to be applied. If the solution isn't delivered in the right way to the ones we are seeking to assist, then all the effort spent trying to resolve it is meaningless as we will not get the expected results.

This stands to be the same with many of the ills that plague our community, especially when dealing with each other. We need to be able to apply patience and tolerance within our everyday lives in order to witness real progress with our relationships. This in itself is not something that takes place instantly. In some cases a great deal of time will pass in order for some to see the benefits and the wisdom of practicing these virtues amongst each other.

Therefore, it will take great patience on the part of those seeking improvement since they will most likely feel the stings from their many failed attempts at tolerating the habits of others. We have to know this is to be expected so we don't fall victim to frustration or despair and give up. We must remember this fact for ourselves and for others because even though our failures may hurt, as long as we're trying we are all growing and learning together.

The Answer:

THERE IS NO QUICK FIX! THERE IS NO FAST WAY FOR OUR ISSUES TO BE REPAIRED! IT TOOK YEARS FOR US TO GET THIS WAY INDIVIDUALLY, AND GENERATIONS FOR US TO GET HERE AS A PEOPLE. SO WE SHOULD BE EQUALLY PREPARED TO INVEST THE SAME AMOUNT OF TIME TO CORRECT AND OVERCOME IT AS WELL!

If you're not in it for the long haul you might as well stop reading now and save yourself the time. Far too often we set

J.G. Robinson

ourselves up for failure by expecting progress too quickly. A good marker for a beginner to look back and see whether or not their effort is paying off should be a year at the earliest. Pick a date like your birthday to look back and do some self reflecting on how you lived in the previous year. If you are pleased with your progress then keep it up you are on the right track!

If the answer is no then don't fret, just make it a point to apologize to those whom you may have wronged or let down. There is no expiration date on an apology! This is a good practice because it takes strength to apologize and you will definitely think twice before you make the same mistake and have to humble yourself before others again!

THE VALUE OF DEPENDENCY

When I was growing up the last thing I wanted was to be dependent upon another individual for anything I needed. **I hated** having to ask another person permission to do something. **I hated** having to wait on them to decide when it was going to happen. **I hated** for them to ask for something in return because they did something for me in the past, and **I hated** for them to throw it in my face if for whatever reason I wasn't able to return the favor. So, trust me when I say I totally understand why many have an issue when it comes to depending on each other to make it in our communities.

So needless to say, when I became an adult making my own decisions and earning my own income, I felt as if I had truly experienced freedom. I came and went as I pleased without having to answer to anyone. I had finally learned what it meant to be independent. This was a great way to live until I met the person I loved and wanted to marry. Suddenly the independence I had worked so hard for and waited so long to get began to be a problem.

Now I had to answer to someone again, and I could not come and go as I pleased anymore. Even though I was an adult, and even though I earned my own income. Later the grasp of responsibility around my life began to tighten even more once I started having children.

I Then found myself being placed on the other side of the equation as now everyone stood around waiting on me, depending on me to make decisions. Or take them to places to buy things and complaining when I didn't move fast enough or take their desires seriously. I couldn't help but ask myself, "how did this happen, and was my life better now or when I was single and independent?"

The truth is it's better to find that special someone, fall in love and raise a family of our own, as opposed to being single and free. Unfortunately, there are some out there who are ill equipped to handle the demanding roles the position of a family member would require of them. This happens for various reasons of finance, maturity, or simply a bad choice in who they married. The responsibility level in taking care of others is huge and not everyone is able to manage these roles.

Therefore, out of frustration and failure at trying to fulfill the expectations and demands of what it means to be a spouse and a parent, many give up and default back to their ways as a single adult. This is the easier road chosen, and it should be noted that it is also the only other option outside of death itself. Although I'm sure if the option of being a child again was possible, many would choose that as well.

Many of us have been misled to believe being independent is the way to be. This is a terrible misinterpretation of how life should be lived. Human beings can only survive together not unlike other species of animals on this planet. In America almost everything we do depends on the workings of another human.

Take the average day of most people we know. First of all, most of us don't even grow the very food we eat, yet we constantly consume three meals a day for ourselves and feed our loved ones.

J.G. Robinson

We do this with these same meals we purchased from some unseen origin. Who started this trend? Even more importantly what would we do if the source of these meals were to stop?

Next let's look at transportation. Few of us can build or even repair the cars we drive to work in everyday or pave the roads on which we drive to get there. Honestly how often does this cross our minds? Also, for those of us who have made it into a higher class of wealth or who secretly envy the wealthy from afar; should take note that many of those extravagant multimillion-dollar estates they live in, would not exist if they had to build them with their own hands.

Lastly, let's not forget the clothes on our very backs. How many of us have even extended so much as a thank you to the person who created that gorgeous wedding gown worn the day you got married? Let's not forget the person who designed those pairs of shoes we love so much. How long would it take to make those on our own?

Some of us couldn't even make a simple Hanes T-shirt if given all the materials and had a gun placed to our head! These items, products and services don't simply fall from the sky, and they definitely aren't owed to us. So, anyone who claims to be "Independent" in this world must really have a distorted view of reality.

We all need each other, regardless of our wealth class, or power status. Human beings always have and always will need to depend on each other to live. Somehow many of us have forgotten this fact especially in our communities. So to speak specifically to our beautiful black women, please stop trying so hard to be independent of black men. This is the exact "opposite" of what our communities and households need to come together.

We love you, and we need you, in more ways than even we are aware of. These "strong and alone" speeches are played out and overrated. Too many of you are growing old alone as a result of the "I can do bad all by myself" philosophy. If you give into this you also consent to spending the remainder of your life going personally unfulfilled. This typically causes women to end up relying

The Black Man's Answer

completely on the lives of their children and grandchildren to bring them partial happiness. This is not the answer.

Come back and take your rightful place in our lives as there are those of us who are struggling without you. We admit we need work, as long as you all understand that it's your loyalty and support we need to succeed, not verbal insults and spiteful ways. So when we fail to meet your expectations (**and believe me we will**) make sure your giving us the necessary treatment needed to keep us strong and focused. As I'm sure many of you have found out by now that the other ways will not get very good results.

To our men, let's do our best to fulfill the roles our women need us to play in their lives. This means getting our act together **before** seeking out a woman for sex. There are many things that can be done on our end long before they become an issue in our relationships. Things such as being employed, staying out of jail, having a place to stay and a reliable means of transportation should be a decent start.

I typically like to say we should have the same things we'd expect another young man to have who is taking our daughter out on a date. This should be considered the minimum requirements when looking to court a woman. Then if we are truly providing for our loved ones properly, we should find that a certain amount of respect can't help but be given to us because we've earned it. This in turn should make trusting and depending on us occur more naturally for those we wish to keep in our lives.

To black men and women together, it will take both of us to stop this phenomenon known as "baby mama and baby daddy drama". This awful trend of common law marriages and children being born out of wedlock has become a common problem in our community. Most cases are usually caused by immature men who were incapable of properly wedding a woman to begin with.

Others are caused by misguided young women who either settled in the relationship due to low self-esteem, or who made a conscious choice to rely on government assistance rather than doing it themselves or making it work with the male who helped get them into the situation.

We must understand that even in a "failed" marriage, the couple's families, and friends get to experience the memories, and traditions that last a lifetime from taking part in a proper union of holy matrimony. Our relatives tend to have much more respect for the individual we love when brought into the family the right way. The children themselves would never have to question their origin or whether or not they were mistakes. It would only take one look at their parents wedding photos and all those questions would be answered.

Settling for a common law marriage, or anything less robs everyone of those very meaningful moments in their lives and the culture overall. Realistically, most of us don't have many of those proud traditional moments to spare in our lives, so why would we skip one on purpose?

The only way to get back to where we belong is to learn how to properly depend on each other again. In a sense, to be married is to be "**dependent**" on your spouse so it's really not possible to be independent and married at the same time. The only kind of independence we should ever strive for is "economic" independence. We must all work together in order to end this poor way of thinking in our culture.

The Answer:

We must learn to interact within our community more. Not everyone is dependable or responsible that goes without saying. However, let's develop safe ways to find those who are, and stand together for what we believe in. Unity is the strongest tool a people can have when used properly. Learning to trust and depend on one another is needed to attain our unity.

Chapter 6
Civic Responsibility

VOLUNTEERING IN OUR COMMUNITIES

I believe I was about fifteen years old or so in high school when I was first presented with the concept of volunteer work. I remember thinking "why would anyone work for free?" What I didn't realize at the time were the benefits and opportunities that could be gained from doing such selfless acts in the community.

Volunteering can come in many different forms. A person could spend their time helping the homeless, cleaning up community parks and playgrounds, or painting the local church or library. It can be used as a great tool to teach your children humility and respect for others and the environment. Depending on how often you volunteer you may be eligible for scholarships and even receive awards from offices as far up as the President of the United States.

Furthermore, volunteering is a great way to network in the community. We have all heard the phrase, "it's not what you know it's who you know" right? Yet it's rare that anyone can actually show you "who" you should meet or "how" to go about knowing those people. Well often the same people who host and sponsor these volunteer programs are the same individuals that own and run the charities and local businesses in the area. In other words, these are the people you need to know! They can give you a job or at a minimum put in a good word, or letter of recommendation for you if needed.

It helps a lot if you can list on an application or state in an interview that you've been volunteering with the company's affiliated non-profit organization. It's even more impressive if you know a couple of the employees currently working for them who could vouch for your character and act as legitimate references.

Volunteering can benefit the community and improve the environment for as little as 2-3 hours a week. This is shorter than it takes watch the Sunday football game lineup, or less than the time our kids spend playing video games. The more we get folks in our communities involved in volunteering, the better all of our lives will be.

The Answer:

Organization at the home and community level is required to enforce this topic. Local churches, schools, and youth centers for instance are a great starting point. This is best done by partnering with groups in the area to make sure the positions are known, and furthermore by publicly recognizing those who have contributed. It would also help to make sure we reward them in a way that encourages more to volunteer in the future.

In any case, the overall goal of volunteering is more productive if done by us for the things we need. If successful, good programs could help reduce the amount of unemployment and provide an alternative for the local youth who don't have many opportunities to gain certain experiences. This is a great thing since we have many teens who are too young for a real job. Yet they are old enough to do drugs, have sex, and join gangs. This should help with reducing those statistics.

CHARITY IN OUR COMMUNITIES

Unlike other topics discussed in this book, this particular issue shouldn't be indulged in right off the back. An individual must first establish a secure financial position for themselves before donating to a worthy cause. However, it's important that we donate first to causes that will benefit our people. It also goes without saying that we should be seeking to establish our own charities as well.

For instance, if there are smart kids in our neighborhoods who we want to see succeed and go further but know it's unlikely to happen. Then we should seek out other adults in the community who feel the same way and see if money or assistance of some sort can be produced to support our own.

Let's assume we are in a perfect world where everyone could be trusted to donate on schedule and be fair in distributing the money raised, there's no telling the progress that could be gained. I personally feel our communities should have at least one fund that everyone can contribute to annually.

This way a certain amount of money and other resources would be available for various community requests. Money can be raised by simple activities such as neighborhood barbecues, bake sales, and car washes on weekends. This can help fundraising and start a charity or non-profit organization for those in the neighborhood.

In time if done correctly, this charity could grant scholarships, help families who've lost their jobs, or property due to a natural disaster. This should give us a means to grant support to whomever we felt deserved it. It could also allow us to host whatever activities we deemed necessary to get things moving in our communities.

In any case, we should not be sitting around hoping and waiting for some business or government entity to notice our community needs a new park, grant our kids scholarships, or help pay for new equipment for our schools. These are all issues the community is capable of providing for themselves with just a little planning and organization. In this day and age with the abilities we have and the limitless access to information available online, we should be able to establish these kinds of support systems for ourselves.

The Answer:

It would be a good idea for us to start at places throughout the community that are already known for hosting fundraisers and see if it's possible it can be taken to the next level. There's no need to reinvent the wheel, and when dealing with money it's always best to use those who have already established a sense of trust within the community. One step at a time, but eventually the efforts of everyone will begin to literally pay off.

COMMUNITY PRIDE

Now that we understand the need for volunteering and charity, the next goal is community pride. I think we can all agree most people like to feel good about where they live. Our community should be clean and safe enough for anyone to relax and enjoy.

This is true not only for us but for those who may need to visit our residences for pleasure or business. Mailmen should have no problem doing their routes, relatives shouldn't be afraid to visit their friends or family, taxi cabs should have no problem coming to the area, and pizza should be easily delivered to our front doors without fear of robbery.

Of course this is easier said than done. Quite a few steps must be taken to get us on the right track. For instance; if there is an eyesore in the neighborhood, let's say an old abandoned house no one has occupied for years, then we need to get together and take action on the situation.

Places like these breed pests such as rats, roaches, and termites. These properties may also have also been used for criminal activities such as drug sales, or possibly even rape or murder at some point. It is without a doubt a negative influence in the neighborhood, only valued by homeless people looking for shelter or other unscrupulous activity. These places absolutely must go!

Combining these issues with the trashy appearance of empty beer cans, broken glass, cigarette butts, and other random trash left on street corners is exactly what drives the property value down and with it our level of pride for the area.

Many of us tend to migrate to these places because they are cheap, and money is always an issue. This is understandable for those of us who don't make much to live on. However, just because it's cheap does not excuse it from meeting basic living standards.

A big part of the problem is that many of us have begun to accept these poor conditions as a black reality and no longer seek to change it. Rats, roaches, drugs, poverty and crime have become part of everyday life in many low income black communities and it needs to stop.

Usually we end up in these situations with the idea that we aren't going to be there long, just temporarily until we get on our feet. Meanwhile years go by and our children get raised in these lousy environments. This often causes them to become victims or products of these environments themselves, thus creating the same factors for them that placed their parents in these communities to begin with.

So ultimately when we finally do get up the strength to move, it's usually to a place not much better than the last. A different location, different people, maybe even different school zones, but with the same conditions that will inevitably produce the same results.

One constant response I receive when speaking to blacks living in housing projects and low income communities about why they aren't trying to take better care of our community is, "Why should we care of it when it doesn't belong to us anyway?" and "What do we look like cleaning up this neighborhood just for others to come and mess it back up?!" I have two things to say to this; *(a)* Whether we clean it up or not they will continue to own it so that's beside the point. *(b)* We should clean up for our own benefit, so our loved ones don't have to live in filth. If others benefit in the process then so be it. Over time this to will work in our favor as blacks become known

J.G. Robinson

for "improving" the community, which is better than being known for destroying it.

The change to improve our environments must come from within us. We could be given the best property in America, our forty acres, reparations, and more, but it won't mean much if we still carry the same flaws and habits on the inside some have developed from living in the ghettos, and projects they previously resided in.

We must develop leaders in our communities. Responsible ones with whom we can trust to take action when needed. Then allow these individuals to represent the rest of us in the political arena and bring issues up with the local governments of our towns. These individuals could be pastors or deacons from our churches, teachers or the high school football coach could work as well.

It doesn't have to be a full-blown politician or college graduate to take action. It just needs to be someone responsible enough to represent us and get things moving to keep the rest of us informed.

Furthermore, the rest of us can do our part by cleaning up our own areas as best as we can to reduce the amount of litter in the community. Yes, we are aware the property value is cheap in low income areas, but that doesn't mean it can't at least be clean. This may not seem like much at first but good habits catch on when seen repeatedly by neighbors and kids. Our children will eventually practice the same thing one day when they get their own homes.

 Then eventually with patience, discipline, and a little unity amongst neighbors, things can change. We can slowly but surely begin to build a "good" community we feel comfortable and content living in. This will be far more beneficial to us in the long run, as opposed to constantly moving to escape the ills of poverty and wandering into foreign suburbs to look for better housing, schools, and family friendly environments.

The Answer:

Let's continue to build on this topic until the term "black neighborhood" becomes synonymous with words like clean and beautiful as opposed to crime and poverty. As always it's going to take plenty of time, patience, and unity to make things work, but it can be done. The first challenge is simply believing the change is possible.

ACQUIRING OWNERSHIP

Ownership is the most important step in acquiring wealth. The most obvious problem we need to address is why many of us don't own the communities we stay in? Buying homes, land, and owning businesses has to become a priority for all of us. Too many of us are content with paying rent or utilizing other people's businesses when we need something. Society has taught us we need great "jobs" to succeed, and college is required for us to have a shot at getting one of these great jobs.

This is a problem because all "jobs" require us to work for someone else who "owns" that business outright. This system of job searching limits us to whatever amount of money they decide is suitable for us, despite the expenses we have at home. Let's also remember when speaking of a college degree, we must factor in that no matter how much effort we exert, time we spent studying, or debt we've acquired on student loans, our degrees cannot be inherited by our children.

Therefore, all the work done to acquire that degree will have to be completed over again by our future generations. This is a great deal for the colleges as they get to profit from one generation to the next. This is not so great a deal for those of us who end up struggling to pay for ourselves and our youth to attend these expensive educational institutions.

However, if we were to own more small businesses we would find not only could we earn more financially, but we would also gain the ability to employ others in our communities. This in itself is priceless! The ability to hire our friends, family, and neighbors would bring much more freedom to us financially and increase the level of happiness and self-esteem overall within our communities. The process would flow much smoother than trying to get hired by some stranger we've never met. Who is more than likely a part of some business we didn't build.

Now many will say this sounds great but there's no way they could possibly afford to start a business especially when it's taken all they've got just to make this month's rent. The thing is, like college, business isn't for everyone. Not everyone is business minded. However, for those of us who do possess the mindset to do so, a couple of things should always be remembered.

For starters, depending on what we are getting into, we must choose something that will generate money for us but not require much to set up and run. To be honest, some businesses can be started for less than what some folks pay for a year of college and can be paid off faster than a lot of these student loans people get tied into from chasing these degrees. It just depends on what skills we have to offer.

For instance a brand new hot dog cart runs about five thousand dollars. Some folks may even be able to buy that with their income tax refund. The annual income received from running a simple hot dog stand can be up to thirty thousand dollars or more, depending on your location and what kind of hours you are willing to put into it. Remember this the next time we hear the phrase "I can't find a job" because many simply don't know this.

Also, don't forget the art of partnerships. If you are looking to make a move but don't have the money, I can assure you someone else is in the same situation. Do a little research and see what's out there. You may end up with several partners depending on the size of your goal. Keep this in mind the next time you see a building, or a few acres of land you'd love to buy because it might just be possible with the right planning.

If done correctly, our goals can be achieved, and we can finally leave worthy assets for our children to inherit. This creates long lasting wealth and passes the torch of ownership from one generation to the next in our community.

The Answer:

It's important we learn to combine forces! So much more can be acquired so much faster if we just use our minds and work together. For instance, if three single mothers who worked as CAN's at a local nursing home got together and pooled their resources, life would be much easier. One mother could be resting, while another mother went on shift, and the third mother watches the kids. Then the positions would rotate as the next mother went on shift and so on. All three could split the mortgage to a nice home with a yard instead of individually paying rent to apartments neither of them owned.

Next a brand-new vehicle could be bought big enough to transport all, while having plenty of money left over to buy a second one and afford any maintenance or repairs needed. This way they could co-sign for each other if needed, which would also increase their individual credit scores as long as their accounts remained in good standing.

The bottom line is if they simply organized and worked together, there would be money left over to do the other things they wanted in life. I'd imagine they probably could even do so without needing government assistance depending on the circumstances. Yet we rarely seem to be able to make it work this way.

Living with others can be difficult and can often result in arguments from everything to who ate certain food in the refrigerator to the use of someone else's toothbrush. Therefore many are hesitant to try group methods and remain stuck in their unfortunate situations. A little humility would help those who fall within this category.

The lack of humility and teamwork is why it's nearly impossible for us to handle simple disagreements between multiple adults in one household. All it would take is one issue that couldn't be reconciled and the whole system would collapse. This often causes everyone to give up and do their own individual things.

So instead, what we usually end up having are three single mothers trying to balance three separate households, driving three different vehicles, and now paying three different fees for daycare since there is no one around to watch the kids.

Furthermore, God forbid the unspeakable happen, like a car accident, or their kids get sick for some reason. Now they are unable to make it to work. So instead of building savings they are now growing debt. Let's be honest with ourselves, does this situation make any sense financially?

Well believe it or not it's more than common in our community then most people realize. There are many who would rather scrape by on independent pride, rather than humble themselves and learn new ways to grow and succeed. We've got to do better at using our minds and working together to make it out here, it's the only way.

THE VALUE OF NETWORKING

As stated before, it's too often we end up struggling within the same vicinity of each other. If we are having trouble with bills, can't find a job, need new clothes for our kids, etc. It seems more likely for some of us to resort to drugs, crime, or government assistance rather than to use our "minds" to figure out a good solution for the dilemma. In many cases our neighbors probably aren't too far from the same situation.

Nevertheless, we would have to swallow our **PRIDE** in order to network with them to achieve a common goal. For example, if we are short on money for food this month we should ask our neighbor if they can help us out, but not for free of course. It should be in exchange for any services they may need help with in their lives.

NO MATTER WHAT SITUATION WE ARE IN WE SHOULD NEVER EXPECT ANYTHING FOR FREE. SOME FORM OF PAYMENT, OR SERVICE SHOULD ALWAYS BE OFFERED IN RETURN TO SHOW OUR APPRECIATION OF THAT PERSON'S GENEROSITY.

These services could be as simple as mowing their lawn or picking up their kids from school on certain days. It doesn't always have to be money. There are many valuable things people can do for each other to make our lives a little easier. Also, this rule doesn't change for family. Family members need to be compensated for the things they do for us most of all. Especially since they have the highest chance of being called upon when something is needed.

The important part for us is to make sure we uphold our end of the bargain. If we are unable to make good on a promise we made, don't be surprised when they refuse further assistance requested in the future. No one is going to assist or network with someone who can't be trusted, nor should they. We must stick to our word if we expect them to do the same and trust us with the responsibility of that task. No one should have to run you down or remind you of a debt you were supposed to repay them.

We may also experience a situation where several people we know may be in need of assistance in life. If organized carefully their combined hardships can give birth to something positive. Now instead of having one person who needs assistance, we have multiple people. This means we all can network and provide services to each other in multiple ways.

Now if one family is without transportation there are now two or more other households that can help them out as opposed to one. This is the way our neighborhoods should work. As the number of folks who need help increases, so should the amount of opportunities for us to help each other.

In time as more of us participate in assisting each other, this will cause the whole neighborhood to interact and be aware of each other's situation which is exactly what networking and building a strong community is all about! If we can get to a point where this happens naturally amongst us in our communities, we will all benefit as a whole.

Then slowly but surely, when pride, shame, and embarrassment is no longer an issue, and we realize people weren't meant to survive on their own. Then we will see networking for what it truly is which is a vital step in achieving our unity.

The Answer:

It's not so much about "who" we network with as long as we take the time to network with others in general. Of course, it would be ideal if we could all network with other wealthy people exclusively. However, when starting off that might not be much of a possibility. Therefore it's best to continue fitting in wherever we can and making sure our wealth and resources finds a way to return home to us.

Chapter 7
Communication

MARRIAGE

I think it's a fair statement to say finding a suitable mate is one of the most important decisions we will have to make in our lives. Everything built from the point of marriage will either succeed or fail based on how successful the union is between us and our new spouse. Therefore, it is of the utmost importance that we make the foundation of our marriages as solid as possible to handle the future issues that are sure to come in life. One of the best tools in achieving this is without a doubt effective communication between the newly wed individuals.

In many ways I feel some of us are lost on how to effectively communicate with our loved ones. When marital problems occur we look for allies to support us in battle rather than seek out someone to help us understand where our partners are coming from.

This dysfunctional habit must change. A large percentage of our culture is filled with broken homes, failed relationships, common law marriages, and heartache. Many of these issues can be traced back to the two original people who created us and gave up on love and each other.

In order to repair our family structure here in America we must first get back to believing in marriage and the benefits that come from it. As men we must learn to communicate to our wives the things we are not pleased with instead of criticizing them as if that will cause the changes we seek.

As women good communication must be returned when received instead of putting up with unwanted behavior. This is more productive than expecting men to just know what you meant or leaving things "better left unsaid" from fear of hurting feelings or ruining the relationship. The trick of effective communication is to be **respectful** in order for the message to be received. This is the only way to ensure a calm sincere conversation is had which will in turn provide a genuine response for us to work with. If the other person still wants to rant and rave then we know it's their own inability to handle the message and no fault of our own.

If folks continue talking to each other without respect it will simply lead to more arguments which typically doesn't benefit either party. If the technique of respectful communication is mastered, I wholeheartedly believe a marriage could survive just about anything, from the death of a child to infidelity.

As long as both parties have decent skills in listening and understanding each other they will find a way to navigate the storm. There are very few situations that can't be compromised, discussed, and ultimately worked out. This also means there should be very few reasons to get a divorce. Stronger bonds and principles should enforce this stage of unity which is indeed the strong union of a loving man and woman.

The Answer:

We need to reestablish the significance and importance of marriage in our communities. Many within the younger generations are questioning it's worth and whether it's needed at all. Let's reaffirm it as the cornerstone of what a strong family should be. However, in order to do so our skills of communication must become greater than what they currently are.

So for all of us who are the friends and family of married couples, let's help them figure it out. Newlyweds often need a different perspective from those who care about them and their well being. Every little bit helps, and once they succeed and prevail through their turbulent moments, this will increase the circle of people who care about our happiness as well.

COMMUNICATION AS PARENTS

As parental figures it's easy to become poor communicators with our children. This usually happens due to us being older, more experienced, more educated, and so on. It can be really hard to accept our children may know or have experienced things we haven't. They may also see things from a different perspective than we ever will. It's important to recognize when they do and actively listen because it happens all the time.

We often demand a lot of respect from our kids in the black community without giving back very much in return. I believe this is partly why some of our kids get to a certain point in their childhood and return the favor by displaying that same lack of respect to others in school. It can be exhibited daily in their own behavior, and in some cases even returning it back to us in our homes. We then retaliate by coming down on them even harder and in some cases even kicking them out of our homes.

Of course, pushing a frustrated young person out into the streets only enhances the damage that's already been done as the child becomes a victim of the street life. The next step from there is usually a life of crime or poverty, and sometimes death. This is not the answer.

In many cases the ghetto's and housing projects can produce kids that have been yelled at, beaten, and cursed at since they were old enough to know their name. Therefore, it should be no surprise when they begin to practice it on others after so many years of poor treatment and conditioning in the home. Unfortunately, there's not much that can be done for those in this category as the entire family structure has collapsed. This is the sad result when the parents themselves are in need of help.

However, for the rest of us I believe our relationships with our children can still be improved. In my experience the best way to strengthen our bonds with our kids is through a healthy line of communication. This should be done with other parents and plenty of interaction with our youth as well.

Furthermore, our ears, minds, and hearts must be open enough to listen to others regarding our parenting skills. This way we can respectfully respond, and if necessary apologize to our children when we've made some poor decisions. This works wonders for both sides because no parent is perfect and therefore every parent has an apology to make to their children for one thing or another. Only when we can freely engage them in this manner, and have them return the same back, can we honestly say we communicate properly with our children.

The Answer:

We must communicate with our children regardless of how awkward or sensitive the situation may be. In fact, one could argue the more delicate the situation is, the more important it is to speak about it. It is imperative we find some means of understanding and relating to them, so we are talking "to them" and not "at them".

PROFESSIONAL RELATIONSHIPS

Whether we are at school, work, church, or anywhere else in public, we should know how to communicate. In my community growing up I saw many people walk into a business and need assistance but not know how to communicate what the problem was they needed assistance with. Then if the person assisting them showed the slightest sign of frustration, or annoyance, they were accused of being rude, or even racist depending on the circumstances.

We have to understand not everyone has the best social skills in society. Therefore, when we do run across someone (and we occasionally will) that doesn't understand how their behavior feels to others, we should always "attempt" to be the bigger person. This can be done by either asking for their supervisor, a different person to assist us, or simply walking away and taking our business elsewhere. Otherwise if we confront and challenge them, things could escalate and cause a scene. This is what we don't want because what generally happens then is we get two equally rude people, both willing to fight it out over a petty and often trivial issue. Once this happens, there is no choice left but for those watching to call the police.

These kinds of situations could be avoided with a little patience and better communication. Remember these altercations could occur at any place or any time. Multiple incidences such as meeting with our child's teacher who rubs us the wrong way. Dealing with a waitress who moves slow and still gets our order wrong. It can occur during instances where we need to ask a boss we dislike for extra work hours, or even speaking with a negligent nurse about the condition of our beloved grandmother.

Over and over again will these challenges come to us, but that's just life. The truth is, the more we go through it, the better we should become at dealing with it. This is important because as a people our success in life, or lack thereof, is often a direct result of how well we interact with those around us. Remember that the next time we experience difficulty with individuals out there in everyday society.

The Answer:

We must continue to strive and push for improved professional communication skills as a whole. Once this has been acquired we can implement it into our own businesses, and develop lucrative networks amongst one another. Which should slowly but surely rid ourselves of the stigma that our businesses, our work ethic, or our sense of professionalism is less than anyone else's.

Chapter 8
Civic Respect

THE ART OF VOTING

The right to vote is something that absolutely must be exercised in our communities. If we ever want to be heard we have to establish a political presence that demands respect. Voting is political power at its lowest level, if properly utilized it can become a very effective tool for us.

In the past, some laws were created to strip us of those rights. Even still to this day there are some who don't know or fully comprehend the concept of why we vote. They don't understand how the system works, or the damage that has truly befallen us due to our lack of political involvement. Our right to vote should be exercised not only at the federal level when electing the President but locally with offices like our county Sheriffs, Mayors, and Judges as well.

We should be well aware of who the local Judges are in our towns. We should pay close attention to the ones that have a habit of sending our youth to prison for life with no parole and how long they have been doing this to folks in our community. We should also make it a point to realize who the Sherriff and District Attorney are, since in many cases these offices act in unison with each other to ensure their future positions come next election.

In any case, we should never ignore those who have power over our communities. We must remember that just because they aren't on television every night, doesn't mean they aren't important. You see without someone to keep the elected officials honest by questioning their motives and methods, we inadvertently condone the things they do that are wrong, or simply unfair.

We must become more aware and responsive to what those in our local offices should be doing because more than often they are the ones guilty of neglecting our communities. This is critical when it comes to disbursement of state and federal funding to help fix our schools, neighborhoods and so on. If not, they will operate in impunity, and only favor those who fund their campaigns for reelection. This typically excludes any of us from the low income side of town.

If there is tax money to be spent throughout the city in the latest budget, we should be fighting to make sure some of that money makes its way to our neighborhoods. If not, we should have no problem calling up our City Councilmen, Treasurer, and anyone else demanding an explanation as to how we got left out.

We must speak up to make sure we are heard! Then based on the action taken by that particular office, can we properly decide whether or not to keep the individuals in their positions, or vote against them due to their lousy performance on our behalf. Otherwise we will always be misrepresented while those from other communities keep ensuring their own interests.

Our ancestors fought hard to earn us the right to vote, they knew the importance and the power of it back then. So how could it be possible so many of us alive today choose to ignore it, or only use it once every four years when it's time to vote for the President? We must do better as a whole in this category in order for things to change.

The Answer:

According to the _Pew Research Center,_ "the black voter turnout rate declined for the first time in 20 years in a presidential election, falling to 59.6% in 2016 after reaching a record-high 66.6% in 2012." In my opinion it would be to the benefit of our people if we were to create a system or a selection process that allowed us to choose and groom our own candidates to run on our behalf. This way we could consolidate our votes behind these candidates and get more political leverage.

This should successfully give us the power we need to push our own agendas through the newly elected officials, or to remove the ones who neglect us or favor others. No one likes a prejudice Judge or Chief of Police who makes their career targeting those in our community. It's time we identified exactly who these individuals are in each of our cities and take the necessary actions to get them replaced. If done properly we can remove them and anyone else in an elected position that doesn't acknowledge our rights and needs as human beings.

CULTURAL ORGANIZATION

It's been my experience that most people (including some blacks) treat our struggle for progress in this country as something that can be completed. As if there is some imaginary finish line that we all should've crossed at some point, and therefore should have moved on from this issue by now. Well I'd be willing to bet those individuals do not understand the concept of capitalism and how the active participation of it, or lack thereof, can affect a group of people as a whole. If they did, that question would answer itself.

No more than we could make it through the day without having to eat, should our race ever consider an existence without a plan to progress as a culture. Even if at a minimum the plan was simply to maintain and hold on to all the progress we've made thus far.

I've met many people who tend to talk about slavery as if it can't come back or doesn't still go on secretly in different forms today. We have to remember slavery existed in other great nations in human history from Egypt, Babylon, Rome, and America, to name a few popular ones. If religion can be considered one of humanity's first systems of government, then slavery can definitely be considered as one of its first economic systems.

The Black Man's Answer

In fact, one could argue that no great nation has ever been built without some form of it slavery to get it started. So it would not surprise me if it were to rise again in the future of humanity. The only question would be is when, where, and "who" will be the poor souls to be subjugated to it.

To become compliant in the position we have achieved in America would be a huge mistake. We must take advantage of what equality and freedom we do have today and seek to solidify it. This should be a common practice of life in general simply because no one is promised tomorrow, not even the nation of America itself. We should strive to go as far as our hearts and minds dare to take us.

During the Civil Rights era we organized several methods to help us "peacefully" combat the injustices we were dealing with during the "Jim Crow" era. Effective tools such as sit-ins, marches, and boycotts showed we possessed the intelligence, discipline, and unity to demand proper respect and fair treatment. Well what happened to that discipline, and unity? Did it dic with our leaders Martin, Malcolm, Marcus, and Huey?

I personally believe the same tools that won us our respect then can effectively be used today. We must insist any business profiting primarily from us but who won't hire or donate anything to us should be boycotted. These methods should be applied in our local areas today as there are still many entities who profit off our community yet give nothing back to us.

Our convenient stores, hair stores, motels, gas stations, pharmacies, and more, are often owned and controlled by outside entities who don't even live amongst us. Let's take the time to discuss these issues amongst one another and form a proper response to them. We should own a broader variety of businesses other than barbershops, hair salons, restaurants, landscaping, and churches in our communities.

This limited amount of commerce can't provide sufficient power, control, or influence for us. We need more! Personally I could never feel secure until we as a people are independently launching our own satellites, running our own wall streets, and curing our own diseases.

We still hold quite a bit of economic power as consumers. Sure the techniques, strategies, and goals may be a bit different due to the changing times but it can still be done. I think the biggest issue is that we don't forget we need to continue striving to make things better. In many ways this is what I believe our strong black leaders were really trying to teach us. It's that we have the power to establish a peaceful wealthy life for ourselves and to never to stop trying until we do so.

The Answer:

According to data published by the *Census Bureau*, "There are about 8 million minority-owned businesses in the United States, according to a 2012 survey, of these about 2.5 million are owned by African Americans. African American owned firms account for about 10 percent of the approximately 27 million in total of U.S. businesses. These black owned firms raked in more than $185 billion in gross receipts and had more than a million people on their payrolls."

We must organize regularly on matters of money, education, politics, healthcare, and so on, the primary focus should be the progression of the culture and its people as a whole. The more we organize ourselves, the less time we spend depending on others or complaining about how someone else did it poorly for us.

DEALING WITH LAW ENFORCEMENT

Since the Civil Rights era and before, the police have by far been the biggest bullies in our communities. They often kick in our doors, unlawfully searching our bodies, homes, and vehicles. It's not uncommon for many of them who work in our communities to frequently address us in a condescending or disrespectful tone. Almost as if attempting to provoke a hostile response on our behalf.

It's also typical for them to railroad us into corners that further incriminate us. They do this while continually manipulating us with elements of entrapment, fear, and intimidation to get the job done. So, to many of us it's amazing how some wonder why the police are so detested amongst the very communities they claim to "serve and protect". I mean why would we protest them if they were truly protecting us and our families?

The system plants their police stations, precincts, and sheriff offices smack in the middle of our neighborhoods under the false pretenses of "cleaning up our communities", or "making the cities safe for all". When the truth is all they want is easy access to low income communities that don't have the time or education needed to know and fight for their rights. These same communities also lack the money or connections needed to take the proper actions in court when those rights have been violated.

Many feel the only true reason for the police in our communities is based solely upon two things; political interests, and job security. The "safety" and "well-being" of our community is definitely at the end of their list of priorities, if even found on the list at all.

Others outside of these disenfranchised communities don't understand this point of view and see those of us who feel this way as ungrateful menaces to society who don't understand what it takes to be a police officer. Therefore, they continually stress the notion that police officers are humans too.

In order to help some folks better understand, allow me to draw this comparison for you; let's say you are a young teenager and the police are really lions prowling the streets of your neighborhood. Now you know these lions have been trained to attack only those who commit crimes. However, you are also aware there have been several instances where these lions have attacked and sometimes even killed people who have committed no crimes at all.

J.G. Robinson

Not only that, but often when it happens the people they typically attack are usually of your culture. What would your reaction be when you saw one of these lions approaching you? Or better yet how would you respond once the lion got face to face with you and began to snarl and bare his teeth? How would you feel or react? Would you humbly submit, run away, or begin to fight for your life? If you're not sure, don't feel too bad, because neither are the scores of black and brown people who get pulled over and approached by them every day.

It's also typical that even when these lions do get the "right" guy who actually did commit the crime they were accused of, this person often ends up being an old friend, relative, coworker, or schoolmate you knew from the past. Who in many cases receives a punishment that far outweighs the crime they were guilty of. In this case let's use a drug dealer as an example as this is a very common scenario in our communities.

It's not uncommon for these (nonviolent offenders) to receive abnormally long sentencing from the courts leaving friends, family, and loved ones to bear witness and endure the pain caused by their absence. You see, for the friends and families of these so called "criminals" the pain doesn't end with the verdict, it begins. In many cases for some of us out there, these "criminals" were paying the bills, helping their families with Christmas, and providing support at times when others did not have it to give.

Yet the authorities still seem to be puzzled about why many of us don't want to snitch on the ones doing this activity. The sad truth is, that by arresting a young drug dealer they didn't solve the problems of the community, in some cases they created more. Once the illegal drug source of income is effectively cut off, folks simply resort to other sources of earning illegal money.

Some of us get caught filing bogus tax returns, government assistance fraud, prostitution, credit card scams, identity theft, or anything that will place an easy dollar in the pocket is fair game. The youth growing up in these environments slowly learn that the

The Black Man's Answer

difference between right and wrong is not as obvious as they had been led to believe. It then becomes just a matter of time before they begin to participate in some of the same activity themselves.

Now the city claims the lions have been retrained and precautions have been taken to discourage and prevent any further misconduct for the townspeople these lions oversee. So now a fresh batch has been released into the streets to patrol again. So, tell me how long would it be before you as a young teen were willing to trust in these "**retrained**" lions?

How long would it take for you to forget about what happened between the lion and your cousin that night? How long before you felt secure in relying upon them for your protection? Especially while they carry that same look in their eye and the majority of your experiences with them weren't of the most pleasant nature?

As you can imagine, significant damage has been done to the overall image of the police in our communities. In many cases the hate between both sides resonates as strongly as it did back in the sixties within the midst of that powerful civil rights footage shown on television. The truth is many of us have never forgotten.

This is primarily why some of us are still hesitant to call the police today, even when we know we need help. We simply feel with so much time, energy, and resources devoted to targeting Blacks, Latinos, and others, how could they possibly be there for our benefit? When asked directly, few of us out there can recall a policeman actually being able to assist them in their time of need or saving their life. Far more can recall being harassed or falsely accused of a situation. It's sad to say but until the positive interactions outweigh the negative between the two sides, I'm afraid the feelings will never change.

It's a hypocrisy within itself how people who don't even live amongst us get to meet downtown and decide what things should or shouldn't be happening in our communities. It's time we stood up to those who would be bullies by exercising our rights, as well as teaching those in our communities who don't know them yet. No

J.G. Robinson

more should we just stand by idly while one of our own gets mistreated.

Regardless of what they may be guilty of we all have rights and part of those rights is the ability to police the police. It will be a different story once the city gets flooded with case after case of police officers who use improper procedures to get arrests. In time the repeat offenders will be identified and weeded out leaving only the "**good officers**" to police the communities, which is the way it should be.

My heart personally goes out to all the black and brown officers who serve on the force. There are many who joined the force to make a difference in their communities and do a damn good job of walking the right path. There are some in my own family who have chosen to serve on the force and I have nothing but love and respect for them. There have also been plenty of good white officers who have been respectful and showed integrity while serving as well so by no means is this an attack on the entire police force as that would not be fair nor true to the ones who do follow the right code.

However, many of us out there do feel there has been an imbalance in the caliber of folks who have been allowed to become police officers and there needs to be constant checks and balances in place to make sure the wicked don't begin to outnumber the righteous ones on the force. Otherwise the people will begin to revolt and at that point it's too late to try and reason with anyone about the issue.

The Answer:

I'm not going to waste time quoting statistics for this particular issue as it has been repeated more than enough for all of us to know things could be better. Don't misunderstand, we as the black community do get that the police are only people themselves, and I would never want to live in a world where there are no police. That sounds like chaos to me which would be terrifying.

However, I do believe the police should carry a higher sense of responsibility since they wield much more authority than the average civilian. I find the notion that we should somehow be equating the lives of law enforcement officers who "**voluntarily**" chose to do a tough dangerous job, with the lives of those killed by them in our community absurd! Especially if there was no probable cause, warrant, or weapon on their person to begin with. Any procedures conducted in this manner are not only morally wrong, but unconstitutional and a violation of our civil rights.

Furthermore, as a police officer if you are that afraid and intimidated by people when doing your job that you have to blow unarmed civilians away (including kids) with your service weapon, then maybe you need to choose a different profession. No one deserves to wear a police uniform when they are slaughtering the very citizens they swore to protect.

I mean what's the point of having, mace, tasers, nightsticks, handcuffs, bulletproof vests, police dogs, riot gas, helicopters, and the ability to call for back up, if you still have to shoot an unarmed 15-year-old dead in the street because you were "unsure" of his capabilities or intentions?

The only answer for this is for the police to put considerable effort into their training and selection of those they entrust to represent them out in the streets. No more should the phrase it's **"better to be tried by twelve than buried by six"**, be used as an acceptable slogan for those in law enforcement. If our boys in blue would simply be fair and respectable when interacting with the community they are assigned to protect, it would go a long way.

We in the black community are not narrow minded nor one sided. We understand there are going to be those of us who break the law and yes, they must be dealt with. As long as those in law enforcement understand those suspects are still our children, friends, and loved ones. So, if they could please exercise some dignity, respect, and humanity while apprehending them.

J.G. Robinson

We would feel much safer and cooperate much more with the police, if we knew our people would be getting their "fair" day in court. As opposed to being judged right there in the street by some cop who had restraint issues. It's our constitutional right to be tried for our crimes and that doesn't disappear just because someone feels intimidated. Any system that could ensure this would go a long way in rebuilding the trust among the citizens in our communities.

Chapter 9
Overall Awareness

ACTIVISM AS A CULTURE

It is important we learn how to react when dealing with injustice. Obviously, activities such as causing riots, looting, or committing arson doesn't achieve much outside of damaging our own neighborhoods. This only serves to make us look like the mindless criminals many out there want to portray us to be in the first place.

I mean let's face it, most business owners have insurance coverage that will more than likely cover the damages from the highly publicized incident anyway. It's also important to mention that many of those business owners don't even live in same communities they profit from.

It's important to understand that if we give into destructive activities, the authorities will have all the reasons needed to pass whatever ordinances or legislature they deem necessary to keep things under control. This is what brings curfews and martial law down upon our cities. We must also point out how the entire police force can't seem to bring order to the situation, yet the news team has no problem getting full coverage of the damage so everyone can witness our chaos and disorder.

This causes the motives and purpose of our actions to become so blurred and distorted that many lose focus on the original reason we rioted in the first place. I've heard from many outside of our culture say how they don't feel there has been a valid reason for a riot or a protest from our people since the sixties civil rights struggle. This shows there are some significant gaps in how we view injustice here in our American society.

I know it's often frustrating when we get held accountable for everything we do, (and even a few things we never did) while others get off on technicalities simply because they knew the right people and can afford a more expensive lawyer. I also understand that for many people in low income communities, they lack the knowledge and resources needed to properly act. This means their frustrations typically go unanswered time and time again. Eventually all the pain and despair finally explode from the community like a volcano in the form of a riot.

Nevertheless this method of expression is still wrong. Rebelling against the system may be a great way to vent, but we've got to find a better way to react that produces positive results for us. We have to take that anger, resentment, pain, and frustration, and use it to our advantage. This way the next time an injustice happens to us, like a black leader getting assassinated, or our kids getting killed and their guilty attacker gets found not guilty, we will have a channel to focus our efforts through.

We must develop a better way of dealing with the unfairness that helps prevent these kinds of things from happening to anyone else in the future. We can use these emotions as an unrelenting drive to unite and stand up for our fallen ones. We have to be able to hold it together and attack those responsible in a way that brings us justice.

In order to come up with such a system this means we should unite and push for new laws to protect our way of life. It's imperative that when dealing with injustice that we understand how different situations may call for different methods of action. However, we cannot allow the situation to add insult to injury by lashing out and acting uncontrollably if something doesn't turn in our favor.

This goes for other elected officials as well. If multiple complaints about bad neighborhoods have gone unanswered or certain police officers continually harass us. Let's make sure it's something we take action on, even if we only call the local news and stir up a lot of controversy for them to deal with. If that doesn't get the job done, then let's make sure we elevate the game play and vote against these individuals the next time around.

The Black Man's Answer

The point is we should never stop until we have attained our goals. Too often when it comes to these issues do we get frustrated or discouraged and walk away from battles we should have continued to fight. Even if we are unable to achieve our goal in one way, there's no reason we can't reorganize and come at it from another angle.

As long as there is someone or something that makes life difficult for us and our community, let's be sure to return the favor. Just remember, when it comes to elected officials, they work for the people not the other way around. There should never be an incident where an injustice is done to our people that does not warrant a consequence of some sort. As long as we assert ourselves in the proper legal manner, there is nothing to fear.

The Answer:

First things first, let's just focus on making sure everyone is aware. The consolidation of opinions is not something we should concern ourselves with. The truth is it's better to have several routes of action as opposed to one central plan anyway. This makes us more resilient as a people. So, let's just make sure we keep each other aware of things that may affect us in the future.

CONTROLLING OUR OWN MEDIA

Every culture of people should have a legitimate source of media. A way in which the culture communicates and addresses it's issues, positive or negative, that may affect them as a whole. In many of our communities this is pretty much reduced to gossip, social media sites, music, and good old-fashioned word of mouth. We own a few radio stations and even fewer television networks. Therefore, when we do receive information important to us, it's rare that we get to be the approval authority on what we hear, when we hear it, or how long it takes for us to hear it. This is not beneficial to us. Allowing others to control our knowledge and flow of information is not a good position to be in.

In most instances, the last person to hear information is usually placed in a helpless or desperate situation. Think back to when you were young, and you were the last one to hear when someone was giving away something free that everyone wanted, did you get one? Or back when you were in high school and was the last to find out someone had a crush on you, how'd that work out?

Now fast forward to being an adult and you were the last one to hear they were hiring at a new company that just opened. Did you get the job? How about if an auction was going on downtown, but you didn't hear about it until mere minutes before it began, did you get to take part in that opportunity? The answer is usually no. More than often those who get the information last end up taking what's left. Usually standing by hoping someone else will share with them, or simply missing out completely.

This unfortunately represents the same condition some of us are dealing with in our communities. This is because we control so little of our own information. We are using "side" methods of spreading news, like pop culture or word of mouth. We end up blindly trusting the current media sources to share the real information fairly with us objectively and unbiased. I personally feel we can and should produce better options for our people.

The Answer:

We need to push for legitimate black media ownership. Much of the media we own is used primarily for music and entertainment purposes, and very rarely reports issues concerning blacks of other regions. If something is happening to our brothers in places like Haiti, London, Brazil, or South Africa to name a few, we should all be aware of it.

Information from abroad increases our awareness and provides opportunities to network both economically and culturally. To rely on other cultures to inform us about ourselves, or our interests is foolish. Once we get used to seeing the news reported based on our own desires and benefits in mind, we will be one step closer to putting the pieces together for our culture.

INTERNATIONAL AFFAIRS

While we've obviously lost our original culture and connection with our native land, there's no excuse for us not developing and forging new bonds with them today. Now this is a step that should of course come later in our cultural evolution. Since we should establish unity within ourselves first and foremost.

At some point we must begin to reach out to blacks of other regions to establish a network of trust and support. Blacks suffering from hardships in Ethiopia, Jamaica, Australia, or anywhere else should be just as much of an issue to us here in this country.

It is also important we do not forget about those here that would make for great allies in our fight for progress and equality. Like the Latino community who are in many ways our brethren of another culture. There's no reason the black and the brown can't combine forces and progress together. It should work especially with Mexico being the immediate southern neighbor to the United States. The potential for both sides to profit and progress is enormous!

If we just take the initiative and get things rolling, there's no limit to what can be achieved. This includes the plight of our Native American brothers as well. I'm sure they could use some help with things on and off the reservations, as well as some additional political backing on their desired agendas.

Truth is there are so many opportunities that it would take all day to list them. I trust that we as a people can see the wisdom in joining forces with those around us to reach a common goal.

J.G. Robinson

The Answer:

We are all one. There really is no other way to say it. When other cultures are oppressed, so are we. When we succeed here in America, our brethren rejoice and imitate us around the world. Whether it's called Jim Crow, or Apartheid, it's all the same thing happening to all the same people and it's time we all understood this issue. The sooner we get over this mental block the better we will all be as a whole.

In a war you need allies, this is just common sense. Even now with the achievements we have in America, they weren't all done solely by blacks. There were several times throughout our history where we were aided by Jews, along with white sympathizers and abolitionists of other cultures as well. These were all strong people who dared to stand up to injustice for all of us.

Therefore, we must not become blind to what could be some great alliances in the future. Remember, "**Divide and Conquer**" was the scheme that got many of us in our poverty-stricken situations to begin with. So, let's reverse it with a "**Unite and Liberate**" strategy. It may sound a little crazy to some, but hey if we want different results we have to try different things.

PRISON SYSTEMS

I am not a fan of America's eagerness to throw people into the prison systems. I feel prisons do a better job of serving other hidden agendas rather than rehabilitating the convicted people they house. I personally believe they are little more than a legal way of reducing a man to a status somewhere between that of a slave and a domesticated animal. In the case of privatized prisons, they pretend to focus on rehabilitation and reform when all they really succeed at is profiting on what is pretty much human storage and slave labor.

118

Furthermore, the fact that most prisons are primarily filled with Blacks and Latinos should be an indicator of foul play within itself. We allow too many of our men and women to fall victim to this system. Yet somehow, we keep tolerating the unsatisfying function of it in our society.

While I totally agree some crimes are unforgivable, and someone has to do something with the people who commit these crimes. I do not see the benefit of creating abnormally long sentences, or making "examples" of people. I don't feel life "without" the possibility of parole is the best answer for the state, or the person convicted.

We must always remember these individuals are people who have families struggling to see them, write them, and praying for them to turn their life around. When you sentence a person to prison, you sentence everyone who was connected to them as well.

I myself have a relative who is incarcerated for life with no possibility of parole for something he did back when we were teens. I've now watched him grow into a middle-aged man, and still going. I know he stands guilty of the crime he was accused and convicted of and he totally admits his fault in what was done decades ago.

However, I also know he was not guilty of committing rape or murder. This is what led me to question the rules concerning the process that got folks sent to prison in the first place. I was always led to believe the punishment should fit the crime. I know now it doesn't play out quite so simply.

The truth is prison serves as a source of income to certain folks. There are those who find stability and even job security based on how many inmates they have occupying those facilities. From the corrections officers, wardens, cooks, medics, and maintenance personnel who run the prison, to the District Attorney, Judge, Probation Officer, Bail Bondsman, Public Defender, and Police Officer who brags about his hefty arrest record. All of these individuals through their livelihood are plugged into the system.

Therefore, how sincere can any of them be about wanting to keep folks out of prison? The minute prison became a source of revenue it

J.G. Robinson

lost its integrity. Consider this, in prison they have commissaries that sale items like cigarettes for instance which are clearly damaging to one's health. Inmates get addicted and the tobacco company gains a lifetime customer.

Inmates can be raped, beaten, and sometimes even killed with cigarettes being used as payment or a form of currency. So one can't help but ask, if they know all this then why haven't they banned cigarettes from all prisons? To find the answer one only has to research the financial statements related to these establishments.

From the food, to the uniforms, to the very soap they are afraid to drop, nothing lacks the potential to make a profit. So to answer the question of who really benefits when a young person gets sentenced to prison for life, the answer is quite a few people. It's probably easier to focus more on who "**doesn't**" benefit, which is usually those of us in the Black & Latino communities.

The Answer:

According to an article published by *The Guardian*, "black Americans are said to be five times more likely to be incarcerated than whites." There is no one way or simple step to solve this issue. Many would argue those rightly convicted by a jury of their peers in a court of law deserve it and if they didn't want to do the time then they shouldn't have committed the crime.

In some cases this may very well be true. However, for our community, we supply a vast majority of the product they refer to as inmates. We cannot, and should not allow such loose interpretations of the law to incarcerate such large numbers of our people. Even when the situation fits, and our youth are fairly and justly prosecuted, we should still take notice and if necessary take further action to ensure they are sentenced fairly. Not only according to the law, but equally to those whom have committed similar offenses in the past.

The punishment must fit the crime. This is something we must act on now! We cannot afford to wait until it directly affects us and our loved ones are in handcuffs. If we don't rise to action when it happens to others in our community, then we can't expect anyone to care when it happens to us.

EDUCATION

Obviously, the cornerstone of any people's progress is their education. In our community this is well known. However, the message is vague and unclear about "**what**" we should be learning, "**why**" we should be learning it, and "**how**" it can be applied to make our lives and communities better.

Knowledge is like any other tool, it's useless to those who don't know how to properly apply it. The public school systems only teach state mandated curriculum in order to meet certain standards. There are many out there in the school systems who are more concerned with misdiagnosing our kids with learning disabilities and passing state mandated tests, rather than teaching them how to succeed in the world around them. In my opinion, there should be no such phrase as "social promotion".

Not to mention the alternatives like private school, or home schooling, are either too costly or too time consuming for the average person to seriously consider. This leaves public school as the only real option for most of the black community.

In most cases the quality of the school increases with the value of the neighborhoods they reside in. So, it's not uncommon for the better schools to be located in the more upscale neighborhoods. This means, good luck to those who dwell within the inner-city limits as the potential for them to learn has been severely handicapped by an ever-diminishing budget.

Next is the higher level of education with the state universities. The knowledge and opportunities gained from attending college can be endless. However, we should keep in mind that typically the majority of degrees earned from attending college are usually only good for a higher level of job hunting. What we should be focusing on is learning how to transition into entrepreneurship. This is something that can be done with or without a degree depending on the type of business one desires. Economic growth in this manner is exactly what our community needs to employ others.

Let's also not forget to mention how the more marketable degrees, are usually accompanied by larger debt. Student loans have become an intimidating factor for those wishing to further their education. With so many hurdles facing our youth, is it any wonder why some of them get frustrated and resort to other things besides pursuing an education?

The truth is, even if there was a way to make college a hundred percent free for blacks everywhere there would still be a certain amount of us who would have no desire in taking advantage of it. The reason is because a "formal" education isn't for everyone. This doesn't mean those who don't pursue it are lazy or dumb, they just have an alternate way of living they have accepted and are fine with.

This can be seen in other cultures amongst the world such as the Amish, Gypsies, Monks, Hippies, Survivalists, and even certain homeless people to name a few. All of which have access to the same opportunities as the rest of us and for various reasons choose to do otherwise.

We as blacks on the other hand don't have much of a "**sub-culture**" here in America. Most of us fall within three categories; **Middle class**, those of us who fit the expected norms of society. **Upper class**, this is for those who have become rich, famous, or who have done something extraordinary like become president. Lastly is the **lower class**, this is typically the group that dwells in poverty or generates an income level close to it. Statistics tell us it's this category that has the highest potential to join gangs, deal drugs, and fill prisons.

Therefore, when a young black person strays away from school the alternative lifestyle chosen is usually associated with crime. It is because of this dilemma that we must get together and formulate

The Black Man's Answer

plans, not only to keep as many as we can in the formal school settings but to provide legitimate options for those who aren't compatible with this way of life.

Our culture consists of both types, so it is a must we build for both. Catering only to those who do well in a formal system of education is a mistake. We have survived in this world long before any school, college, or university existed, so it is ridiculous to act as if that is the only method of survival for us today. It is our job to create a system within ourselves that utilizes those of us who do not conform well to the rules of society. Otherwise, these same folks will be used as pawns and ultimately profited on by others outside of our culture.

The Answer:

According to data published by *The Journal of Blacks in Higher Education*, "in 2008 19.6 percent of all African Americans over the age of 25 held a college degree. This figure has in-creased significantly from 13.8 percent in 1996 and 11.3 percent in 1990."

To those of us who have been fortunate enough to graduate from these prestigious institutions, we should really take the time to reinvest some of that knowledge and wealth back into our communities on some level. Perhaps this will provide some suitable options for those looking for other avenues in life.

If not, then the burden will fall onto the uneducated people themselves to figure it out. I personally do not recommend this as it would be like telling a lost person to "figure it out" and stop being lost on their own. Now how effective would that advice actually be?

J.G. Robinson

Chapter 10
Patriotism

OUR ALLEGIANCE

I can say personally for me the message has always been confusing about to whom we really place our allegiance. I have made a living in the military and have witnessed firsthand how there are those of us out there who don't place as much pride and ownership in this nation as others when it comes to showing patriotism or honoring our own fallen warriors. This is sad because blacks have been giving our lives freely for this country since the revolution itself. I've said it once and I'll say it again;

"FROM THE COTTON FIELDS TO THE BATTLE FIELDS, WE'VE PAID THE PRICE TO BE HERE!"

So, it's very important that we don't allow anyone to make us feel as if we are anything less than proud Americans as well. We have as much right to wave the red white and blue as anyone else, and should gladly put our deeds up against any other culture that lays claim to citizenship here.

Yet somehow it doesn't seem to work that way. For instance, I have on many occasions met other families, and businessmen in my travels who heard I was in the military and instantly shook my hand and told me "thank you for your service" as a sign of respect for the job I did. Then I in turn responded with a smile and humbly said, "thank you sir or ma'am" returning that same respect and continued on my way feeling good about myself and the choices I'd made in my life.

However, when I go back home to visit my own family, or when I meet other black citizens while dressed in uniform, I am lucky to receive a simple "hello" from them let alone any acknowledgement of my military service. Where's the pride for "**OUR**" warriors? I must have gone to more barbeques and family cookouts than I care to remember on Memorial Day, Veteran's Day, 4th of July, etc; and very seldom have I seen a black family play the national anthem before starting an event or speak a few words on behalf of a fallen servicemember from their family. It's rare that I recall seeing anyone even place an American flag out front while celebrating these days.

Usually we just say the blessing, pass the food, and crank the music. This is great but where's the message or purpose that shows what we are having this party for? If done this way the holiday is reduced to just being another day to party, which could have happened on any ole day for any ole reason. It will not have any value or significance.

However, if we take the time to honor **OUR** country, **OUR** warriors, and **OUR** history, in a way that fits us. Then these events would no longer be referred to as just mere cookouts and barbeques. Our children will begin to remember that this is the one day of the year the family gets together to show patriotism. They could honor grandpa as the veteran of the family or visit the national cemetery where a beloved family member was buried. It could also be as simple as watching movies like the "*Tuskegee Airmen*" or "*Glory*" to make us all feel proud of our contributions to this nation.

Whatever way we chose to celebrate would now become a time to cherish and display our sense of patriotism for this country that is our home. Once this happens, I believe we will have established something that can grow to become a tradition for our future generations. This will slowly but surely develop what should have been there anyway, which is a strong heritage and sense of patriotism amongst our people.

J.G. Robinson

The Answer:

Our home is our home. Regardless of how it came to be that way, it is our home nonetheless. So unless we have plans to migrate elsewhere before we die, we might as well get used to it. We were born as Americans with an obvious lineage from our African ancestors. We are a part of America's society and an irreplaceable part of the nation's history. We live everyday as Americans, and we will die as Americans. I don't really see anything else to it.

Chapter 11
Health

LEARNING TO DIET

A healthy well-balanced diet is something many of us still struggle with as a people. It is important we examine our eating habits and make improvements where needed. First let's start with the consumption of soul food in our homes. As a southern black male, I've seen many of the same dishes in the homes of my people. Entrees such as fried chicken, potato salad, collard greens, corn bread, barbeque ribs, etc.

Now there's nothing wrong with these meals, in fact they are delicious, and I continue to eat them to this day. However, they are often prepared in ways that make them high in fat, cholesterol, sodium and other undesirables. We must learn how to reduce the amount of non-essentials being added to our meals.

For instance, does the chicken have to be fried, and if so what are we frying it with? Some of us out there are still using lard as a cooking agent. How about the potato salad? How many ingredients do we place in this dish? Depending on the size of the dish an entire jar of mayonnaise can be used to complete it and most of us will even go back for seconds. The collard greens maybe the healthiest dish on the menu, but in most cases many of us couldn't describe what vitamins and minerals they contain if any that benefit us.

Items such as cornbread, sweet tea, and yams often contain so much butter and sugar between them it's scary and we haven't even made it to the desserts yet! The traditional sweet potato pie, cobbler, homemade banana pudding, etc; can really pack on the pounds if we're not careful. Nevertheless many of us will go back for seconds, and sometimes even thirds!

J.G. Robinson

I don't think we have any idea of how many calories we end up consuming during these meals. Taking the time to refine some details during the preparation could help a lot in reducing the amount we take in. Especially since most of us plan to continue eating these items for the rest of our lives.

Second is giving into fast food. It's understandable that fast food may be a common option for some, since many of us come from single parent homes. It's typical for one parent to work multiple jobs and therefore not have the time required to make full course meals every day. However, Chinese takeout, hamburgers and fries, or the local taco stand, shouldn't be on the menu three or more times a week either. Even if time is short there are other alternative methods to making decent meals that don't involve fast food.

Not only are most fast food restaurants high in calories but it can become an expensive habit if done too often. I'm not saying we all have to become vegans, but let's take a look at how we can do better there are options that will be reasonable for the amount of time and money we have to work with.

This leads us to the next issue which is a general lack of knowledge on how to cook healthy food. Granted, this subject probably requires the most work being that it takes time to educate oneself properly on the best way to prepare meals. However, it is a necessary step to prepare food the right way, so they don't contain as much salt, sugar, fat, cholesterol, etc.

Also, fresh organic foods can be expensive in their own right. Let's make sure whatever new nutritious choices we end up with feel just as good to our paychecks as it does to our bodies. It's important to know and teach to everyone that these meals can be prepared in healthier ways and continue to taste terrific.

Next on the list is portion control. As I have already mentioned. It's not uncommon for us to go back for seconds. Sometimes it may not be what we are eating that's the problem, rather than the fact we are simply eating too much of it. Going back for seconds is not a bad thing if done once in a while. It shouldn't be done after every meal though. It also makes no sense to get seconds if the first helping we had was literally spilling over the edge of the plate.

Only reasonably sized servings deserve second helpings of equal or less size. Typically In our homes we encourage eating big because food comforts us and brings us together. It's often considered a compliment to the cook if we clean our plates and go back for more. Unfortunately this has taught many of us to overeat. Overeating is a common problem for many Americans not just our community. Therefore, we must remember that in general the average portions we eat per meal and the ones given at restaurants are usually more than enough.

We must pay attention to this especially when eating out. Let's face it, restaurants are a business and are therefore interested in the same thing any other business is interested in…making money. Our health is not a concern for them. In fact the only time it becomes a concern is when a customer claims food poisoning or when they are competing with another restaurant for more business.

For instance, if some competitors across the street from a rival restaurant introduce a hot new low-calorie product that actually taste good, then you had better believe the other restaurant is going to try and answer the challenge. This is done however for financial reasons more so than their concern for the health and well being of their customers.

In fact, even when dealing with alcohol, the bartender has the right to cut you off if he or she feels you have had too much to drink. Regardless of how much money you may have, you're forced to stop and if you disagree the police can be called to force you to do so. It's too bad this rule is not enforced in fast food and "all you can eat" restaurants.

Countless times I've personally sat at a buffet and watched an obviously obese person walk back up to the counter again, and again for more food. Why do we allow this? For some reason our society frowns on a drunkard and pacifies a glutton. In any case my point is we must make a healthy diet our own conscious decision. The size of our meals and how frequently we eat them must be monitored in some way if we ever expect to get this issue under control.

The Answer:

According to data published by the *American Heart Association,* "non-Hispanic blacks age 20 and older, 44.4% of men and 48.9% of women have Cardio Vascular Disease, and in 2009 Cardio Vascular Disease caused the deaths of 46,334 black males and 48,070 black females." Let's do what we can to make dinner time less dangerous.

There have been many fabulous alternatives invented for traditional home cooked meals these days. It's worth experimenting with some new techniques to find out what works for us and our families. Otherwise we will remain stubborn and stuck to the same old ways that have proven to cause African Americans many health problems in our old age. Let's make an honest effort to clean up our habits on this issue. Otherwise we will stand guilty of perpetuating a certain "cultural ignorance" concerning matters of our own health.

DRUGS & ALCOHOL

Lord knows the average African American has had their share of issues concerning the effects of drugs and alcohol in our communities. So, I don't think there's a need to reiterate all the sad statistics that get thrown in our faces about our people regarding this issue. I know statistical information is meant to make us all more aware of our status and personal situations.

However, I personally feel in certain cases publicizing this information for the whole world to see inadvertently reinforces negative stereotypes concerning our people. This can potentially lower the self esteem and confidence of our people as a whole and alter how we are perceived by those who hear it, even if only at a subconscious level. Also, many of us in our communities have been hearing these statistics for so long that most don't even care anymore.

Therefore, I think it far more productive to discuss "why" we have become reliant on things such as drugs and alcohol to begin with. What I have found at the core of most blacks who frequently used and abused these substances was that they were all in some way depressed and frustrated at how their lives were turning out. They turned to drugs as a way to self medicate and relieve themselves of whatever stress factors were occurring in their daily lives.

So, our enemies aren't necessarily the drugs, the people who brought them here, or those who enforce the laws around them. The truth is, if we were truly happy and content with ourselves and our lives, we would have never picked up the drugs to begin with.

The real enemy here is stress and depression. Drugs and Alcohol have simply become the easy way to suppress the issues for those who don't have the funds or resources to get better professional help. In order to combat this issue, we have to identify what circumstances are causing such depression amongst our people in the first place. Then we can discuss what can be done to reduce these factors as much as possible. Only when we've taken these steps can we begin to decrease the amount of drugs and alcohol consumed amongst our people.

The Answer:

According to data published by the _National Institute on Alcohol Abuse and Alcoholism,_ "Blacks and Hispanics experience higher rates than whites of recurrent or persistent dependence with alcohol. Furthermore, the consequences of drinking appear to be more profound for Native Americans, Hispanics, and Blacks."

We must find better ways to support and comfort each other emotionally. Too often do we believe we are strong, tough, or don't need anyone. Well that's just pride talking!

If the number of people we could trust and depend on were to increase, then almost simultaneously would we begin to see the

J.G. Robinson

amount of deaths and incarceration behind drug and alcohol related incidents slowly fall. We cannot afford to focus so hard on the smoke that we forget to put out the fire. Let's concentrate on teaching this to our youth so they have a better chance of avoiding this obstacle.

EXERCISE REGULARLY

It's actually somewhat surprising to me that we could use improvement in this area because so many of us are so gifted when it comes to athleticism. We perform impressively in most professional sports, and to be honest I can't even remember the last time the titles of fastest man and woman on the planet weren't held by members of the ebony race.

However, there are still those of us who aren't as blessed as others and need a little encouragement getting out there and breaking a sweat every now and then. Many of the adults I saw growing up in my neighborhood (the ones trying to live right) never had the time to work out or exert energy into anything that wasn't making them money.

Therefore, when a chance arose to relax that's exactly what they did, and who could blame them? Most of them were single parents trying to make ends meet, or grandparents trying to help their own children out of some hopeless financial situation. Others were simply people who had to work two jobs because they didn't finish school and minimum wage only paid so much. So it's not hard to see why exercise doesn't necessarily make it on our daily "things to do list".

Nevertheless, with all that being said it's still a major factor in our overall health and has to be recognized. It's really just simple common sense. The better we take care of our bodies the longer they will last and the happier we will be. Let's also be honest about one thing here. Getting visibly fat or obese should not be the only indicator or motivation to start exercising. There are many of us who feel that because our partners still find us sexually attractive there is no need for anything more. This is false!

To begin with sexual attraction and physical health are two completely different topics that should never be confused. Many people aren't even capable of reaching certain levels of obesity if they tried. It's simply not in everyone's genetics to do so. Meaning it's not necessarily something to brag about if you've only gained thirty pounds instead of a hundred like some people you've seen.

It's also not a good practice to compare ourselves to others either. We must remember another person possesses a completely different genetic makeup or could even have a medical condition that effects how they lose, gain, or carry their weight that we are unaware of. The same could be said for a morbidly obese person who is looking to have a perfect six pack and chisel toned body. It simply may not be genetically possible.

So instead let's strive for the important things like increased energy, better flexibility, easier breathing, longer stamina and endurance. All are indicators of being in good shape. These are reasonable goals for increasing the overall longevity of our bodies and ultimately our lives. Otherwise we run the risk of working ourselves to an early grave. Or we allow idleness to take over to the point where we become disabled and lie around all day collecting disability and social security checks. Which is sad but ultimately the future of many of us if we don't do something to prevent it.

The Answer:

We love sports, and many of us are extremely athletic in the beginning of our lives. Unfortunately, the problem usually arrives later in life passed the age of thirty. This is when all many of us do is eat sleep and work. It's from this point on that we really start to put on the weight and suffer from conditions like heart disease, high blood pressure, hypertension, diabetes, and so on.

We must find a way to remain active as long as we can. Finding an excuse to sweat and get our heart rate up regularly is half the

J.G. Robinson

battle. The other half is continuing to do so decades later. Those who succeed will more than likely enjoy a healthier body for a longer period than those who don't. This coupled with good dieting is the best natural tool we have for slowing down the aging process.

MENTAL HEALTH

I find it disturbing that for all the trials and tribulations we African Americans endure in our lives, it seems so few of us seek out or receive counseling and therapy for our issues. We simply cannot afford to neglect our mental health. There are too many traumatic events that occur within our lives to do so.

The first argument most people will make when therapy is suggested is usually about the money. Yes it's true that licensed professionals aren't cheap. Therefore those of us who lack the cash to afford treatment must learn to seek out other ways to get the help. Sometimes self help groups can be found in the local area. Perhaps the Pastor at our local church should be able to offer counseling and probably have a few more tricks up his sleeve to help us out depending on the situation.

Also, let's not forget close friends and relatives. Many times, without realizing it our friends tend to act as our "cost free" counselors anyway. Unfortunately, in many cases good friends can be hard to come by. This means that those of us who are lucky enough to have a reliable friend who can listen and understand us, should do whatever it takes to keep those people around.

We must also be sure to return the favor of counseling them when they are in need as well. Failure to do so may result in a weakened relationship between the two of you or even the loss of that friend altogether. This tends to happen once they realize the comfort and understanding they give isn't going to be returned when they need it.

The second argument made by folks against going to therapy will probably concern the time. The harsh reality is that a single mother working two jobs hardly has enough time for herself let alone multiple hour-long therapy sessions throughout the week. However, there are ways to carve out a moment of time for our mental well being. Not saying it will be easy, but we should try to work out something that will allow at least one session per month. It may not be as much as we like or need at the time but a little is better than nothing in the long run.

The last argument most people make will usually involve some level of pride or embarrassment from having to see a psychologist. Most people don't like the stigma that comes from getting mental health treatment and our community is no different. It's often viewed by many in society that receiving mental health services is the sign of an unstable person or that the individual is too weak to hold it together on their own.

Contrary to this belief it is actually the opposite. It takes a strong person to admit they need help in life. There is nothing wrong with this. If only we could see how trying to be so strong and independent is destroying us piece by piece, we could reverse the damage that's been done. In any case, whomever we decide to trust with our emotions we must always remember two important things;

1. WE MUST BE COMPLETELY HONEST ABOUT THE DETAILS OF OUR SITUATION NO MATTER HOW EMBARASSING OR UNFLATTERING THEY MAY BE.

2. WE MUST BE PREPARED TO HEAR THAT WE MAY HAVE BEEN WRONG IN OUR ACTIONS DESPITE HOW GOOD OUR INTENTIONS MAY HAVE BEEN.

If we don't remember to apply these statements to ourselves, it won't matter who counsels us since it won't be effective unless we provide all the information needed. So if we're serious about

J.G. Robinson

healing, we have to go all in. Otherwise it's not even worth the effort.

The Answer:

According to the Health and Human Services Office of Minority Health, "African Americans are 20% more likely to experience serious mental health problems than the general population. We suffer from health disorders such as major depression, ADHD, suicide, and PTSD because we are more likely to become victims of violent crimes. African Americans are also more likely to experience factors that increase the risk for developing mental health conditions that lead to homelessness in which we make up 40% of the population."

In order to take the stigma out of visiting a psychologist, we must be educated on the benefits of going and the consequences of not doing so. Many of us feel that because we have seen others in our community handle it without help, that we should be able to do the same. This is not necessarily true. Take being a single mother for instance. There are so many women who have been able to overcome the issues associated with being a single parent and that's fantastic.

However, we have all heard some of the terrible tales of those who couldn't handle the situation and ended up getting their kids taken by the state. Or the sad women who fall victim to things like prostitution, drugs, or suicide every year. Even still worse than that are the unspeakable situations where a parent actually loses control and kills their own children. We've got to do whatever we can to ensure these kinds of things don't happen to us.

Efforts must be combined to make mental health services more affordable, available, and acceptable to our communities. If it can't be arranged via state or federal government services, then we will just have to establish something amongst ourselves. We can do this using our local churches and community organizations, but either way it must be done.

SPIRITUAL WELL-BEING

Spiritual health can pertain to many things. I myself will use it to reference the wholesome things in life that make us happy, content, and leave us with a satisfied sense of fulfillment. These are the things that give our lives meaning and ultimately a purpose. It is important to be aware of this fact because denial of our spiritual side can lead to depression, anxiety, and possibly even suicide.

Some of us use our jobs or careers as our identity and self worth, while others may use their children as their driving focus in life. Even still some use religion and the church as the almighty force that keeps them grounded. There really is no wrong way to find fulfillment.

Just as long as we understand that it needs to be established for everyone at some point in their lives. As their loved ones, we should give them the freedom needed to figure it out. I've personally known so many blacks who held incredible talent, only to let it all slip away as the years passed. I must have seen and heard of scores of talented people such as musicians, athletes, artists, poets, etc, who just faded away into mediocrity or worse.

I myself am writing this very book not knowing if it will ever go any further than my own desk. Yet here I am, writing to my people about how we can rise together. Why, because it fulfills me and gives purpose to my small existence in this world. It's all done on my own time and dime. It's also important to remember one crucial point when pursuing your purpose, which is the passion that fulfills you, does not "have" to make you money.

Just consider it a bonus for those of us who are lucky enough to get paid and be fulfilled at the same time. So from now on if we should ever start to feel trapped in our daily routines. Let's be sure to take a step back, breathe, and think about that special thing that puts a smile on our face. For those of us who haven't found it yet, let's make sure we take the time to establish this new source of

J.G. Robinson

fulfillment. This will ensure happiness and good spiritual health among ourselves and others.

The Answer:

Many of us search for a purpose and instinctively know church alone cannot provide it. Most have no clue on how to fill the void existing within us. There are some who doubt a spiritual side of humanity even exist, and therefore neglect it altogether.

We must never stop searching for the things that make life worth living. If we do, then we shouldn't be surprised when our life "isn't" worth living. Finding our purpose is one of the greatest journeys in life, and a critical part of one's spiritual health.

The answers we seek are usually hidden from everyone including ourselves. We must remember there is no clear path or proven steps to achieve satisfaction in this world. If we are aware of how important it is to solve this riddle called life, then we stand a chance of finding true peace within ourselves.

MEDICAL CARE

Everyone at some point in their life will need medical care. Our community is no exception. In the past blacks were handled poorly by the medical industry here in America. Many years ago, it was not uncommon for us to be used as guinea pigs or become victims of malpractice.

As time went on this bred distrust of those who practiced modern medicine within our community. This caused many of us to rely on the use of home remedies as opposed to being checked out by practicing physicians. Many of us in the southern United States still have elders who swear by products like Castor oil, Epsom Salt, and other random creams and ointments. To be honest, I'm still not sure what medicinal value they actually contained. Most I felt acted as placebos for folks like my family who couldn't afford good health insurance to get proper medical treatment. Looking back at it, I think a large percentage of it was just comfort and attention to help me get through until the virus or bug passed through my system.

Today most of us have gotten more comfortable and for the most part use the same facilities as anyone else needing medical assistance. Affordable health care should always be a topic of concern amongst our elected officials. Medicare and Medicaid are great, but they only cover so much. President Barack Obama knew this and did what he could to pass "The Affordable Care Act" while he was in office.

In an ideal world we could ensure we were able to do our own medical research. This way we would have access to all the plants and substances U.S. Customs forbids us to bring into the country from other regions of the world. We could produce or own hospitals, pioneer our own pharmaceutical advances, and decide what diseases to take on that have become an epidemic to our people here in America and abroad.

This way we wouldn't have to debate whether diseases like AIDS, Ebola, Sickle Cell, or Malaria, were honestly attempting to be cured. Nor would we have to wonder if some rich individuals outside the culture were simply conspiring to get richer off the profits from selling us the medications. Or even worse is to worry if they were using these and other pandemics as a tool for genocide upon our people.

It would be nice to eliminate all the distrust and speculation I've heard expressed from many in our community regarding the medical industry and its practices. Unfortunately, this will never happen as long as we feel like we are at the mercy of someone else's decisions. As recently as a few months ago I heard there was still suspicion of "organ stealing" going on with the poor and homeless individuals that get reported missing and never to be seen again.

I also know many fellow blacks who refuse to give blood simply because they are not sure what is being done with it once it leaves their sight. I'd like to say I was making this stuff up but I'm not. I'd also like to tell them all they are wrong, but the truth is I don't know that for sure either. The one thing I do know is we would all wonder a lot less if we were involved in more of it ourselves.

The one thing we can control however is our own personal health. We must make sure we take the time to schedule our medical appointments regularly as opposed to being stubborn about the situation. Our pregnant women, newborns, annual checkups, exams, dental, and so on. All of this and more are needed to ensure our well being.

In low income black communities especially, as many individuals either can't afford the insurance or aren't responsible enough to make the appointments and properly maintain themselves. Better attention to ourselves medically will help us control and reduce issues that plague the community like the spread of sexually transmitted diseases for instance. Our people will without a doubt, live safer and longer if we increase the level of participation at this level.

The Answer:

As long as our health is being monitored and not neglected there is hope. Time and money must be set aside for us to ensure we are taken care of medically and aren't allowing years to pass by without seeing a doctor or dentist. If practiced properly it will become routine and our youth, having grown up with memories of frequent visits, will carry it on to the next generation.

Chapter 12
Discipline

THE RESPONSIBILITY OF OUR MEN

No plan created will succeed without maintaining the proper discipline to see it through. With that being said, the problem for some of us brothers today is the lack of a plan to begin with. I challenge my fellow brethren to set some reasonable goals for ourselves. Develop traits and values that will make our women proud to call us their sons, brothers, husbands, fathers, or uncles.

At the moment it seems we as African Americans don't currently have much of a rite of passage ritual for us to enter adulthood, but that doesn't mean we can't develop some new ones. We can be strong and respected in any position but we have to establish our own sense of self worth first. It will be easier for others to believe in us once they see how much we believe in ourselves.

Let's make sure this much is achieved before we even think of attaining a mate. Our women need us to be strong and by their sides in life. When things get rocky they should be able to look to us for support, comfort, financial security, and safety if needed. If not then we have no right to be angry when they find it from other sources such as their sisters, mothers, coworkers, best friends, or men of another culture.

It's important that we take the time to ensure we only reproduce with women whom we deem worthy of marriage and motherhood. One of the worst things our community has to deal with are males who carelessly impregnate women they had no intention of being with in the first place. The next thing would be the men who created life with no financial means of providing a decent life for his loved ones. These kinds of men recklessly complicate the lives of the female, the new child, and whatever future man that tries to make an honest family out of them.

It should become a common rule amongst brothers to have two things when dealing with our women; birth control, and a stable source of income. So many men claim they want to be leaders in their homes. However, true leadership starts with ourselves first. If we can't achieve these simple standards beforehand while we are single, then we have no right to try and demand that kind of respect from our women.

Our young black males must get back to being MEN. Too many of us believe that being the head of the household is something that is owed to us which is simply not true. We have to earn it! Therefore, we must bust our butts to stay on track to becoming someone worthy of being respected from those around us. There is a basic path every man should have as the backbone of his foundation. The code is as follows:

EDUCATION>LIVELIHOOD>MATE>FAMILY>COMMUNITY

Now each milestone doesn't necessarily have to be achieved in this exact order. However, this is the sequence in which they are most easily accomplished for most. Any man who successfully completes and maintains these virtues will never find his manhood in question. As he will have done for others as well as himself, and his respect and admiration will be plentiful. So much so that even in death their names will ring with great respect when mentioned amongst the living.

Our greatest leaders, Martin Luther King Jr, President Barack Obama, and others whether they knew it or not followed this simple formula. We too can all do this very same thing in our own special ways, but we have to have the discipline to do so. Once enough of us rise we can teach the rest and eventually achieve true peace & unity.

The Black Man's Answer

The Answer:

A certain percentage of black men who escape these stereotypical pitfalls often do so by forsaking their culture. They change everything from the music they enjoy, to the way they speak, and in some cases end up marrying outside the race. By the time they have achieved their goal of success, they are so far removed from the rest of us that they are no longer viewed as representing our culture anymore.

It is this type of brother we refer to as being the sellout, Uncle Tom, or House Negro. Now in most cases, it's probably not even true that they don't associate with their own anymore. However, I believe this notion occurs simply because of their perceived lack of allegiance to their own people.

We must find a way to succeed that does not cost us our identity as the proud black men we are. This can be achieved by working together with each other to reach our goals. This is where the discipline will matter the most. We must learn to "hear" each other and not challenge our fellow African American brethren every time there is a disagreement.

Everyone can't be in charge, and someone is going to have to put their ideas aside for the time being to support the brother who has a vision big enough for "everyone" to share. We can do our part by making sure he has the resources needed to make it happen. This is how order is maintained in any organization. This way if the person leading is found to be untrustworthy, then we can replace him with someone better and move on.

Once we have mastered using this technique as a community and practice it regularly to make decisions, we will find ourselves easier to rely and depend on. This should make networking, teamwork, and ultimately unity amongst us all, less of a dream and more of a reality.

J.G. Robinson

THE REPONSIBILITY OF OUR WOMEN

The beautiful women of the ebony race have endured so much. We cannot blame them for many of the choices they have had to make in this world. Much of it was done out of the need to survive. However, we now need more than just mere survival. It is now a question of progress. We need to do better as a whole and we cannot do so without our women by our side. They are by far our most valuable assets.

As our women we ask you do your best to believe in your black males. Not just on a romantic relationship level but in all aspects of life. Your brothers need to hear you're proud of them in every way. There is nothing better for a son than to know he is pleasing his mother. So say it aloud and show it as often as possible because he will carry those same emotions from your relationship to his new bride one day. This goes for all the other important male relationships our women may have.

Let your fathers, uncles, nephews, brothers, male cousins, and sons know you love and value their relationship. This will go a long way to building the good strong bonds needed to solidify the family as a whole. Say it aloud and if possible in front of other friends and relatives so they can see what a healthy relationship looks and sounds like.

Too often we expect to hear loving endearing sentiments from our friends and family without realizing that we don't give very much out to anyone ourselves. It's true some things may be left better unsaid. However, letting the males in your family know they are cherished and appreciated, should not be one of them.

Also, as black women please do your best to wait for marriage before beginning to have children. You are beautiful creatures so of course your black princes are rushing to claim you. Just please try to

The Black Man's Answer

make sure they exhibit proper signs of manhood and not just mutual attraction at that moment. We need our sisters to focus on the "future" of the family a little more, and to get swept up in emotion a little less. As black women you have the power to demand whatever you may need from your potential mates to verify if they are worthy of your love. All we ask is that you use that power to ensure a good future for yourselves, the children you will produce, and your future husband as well.

We can end this awful trend of baby mama's and baby daddy's, provided our females demand men properly respect them before losing their virtue or birthing their children. It won't happen overnight of course but like any other trend or change, if all commit properly, it will begin to occur more frequently. However, it's going to take some discipline to make this stick. Yes, there will be frustration as you will lose out on some cute guys who don't care to wait or take life seriously. However, don't worry because those are the kind of guys who typically leave and weren't going to stay for long anyway. This would have happened no matter how hard you tried to keep them.

This is the only way to separate the men from the boys. This way you can look forward to things like planning a wedding, honeymoon, or baby showers, rather than filing for child support on some irresponsible guy who probably was never committed to you to begin with. This should also reduce the chances of you being involved in domestic violence as well. It should help since the probability of you being stuck with someone who feels like they "**settled**" because they got trapped by a pregnancy or couldn't do any better should be greatly reduced.

Overall, this should increase the chances of the "good" black men being able to meet the "good" black women and achieve stable lives and households together. This in turn will improve the communities we live in by allowing peace, and happiness to reign in our homes. This will take effect on a broader scale not just for the wealthy members of our community. This type of planning is

J.G. Robinson

necessary to decrease the amount of unbalanced, single parent, and sometimes dysfunctional homes so many of us have experienced in our communities.

The Answer:

Ladies, we need you to have the discipline to say no until he proves he wants to seriously get involved with you. It's also a good idea to make sure your married before you birth any kids from a man. No matter how charming he may be or how much you want him to hang around. These things may seem old fashioned, but they still do a great job of eliminating guys who don't have your best interest at heart. This helps your chances of finding a real man who is serious about love and support as that's what our sisters truly need in their lives.

Also, once our women have "**finally**" gotten around the whole relationship and finance curve. Then we can really focus on the things we need our women to focus on, which is success and self-fulfillment! Our women should be able to focus on themselves, develop hobbies, build professional relationships and organize amongst each other. This would help to create change by diversifying our culture and capabilities here in America and abroad in other nations.

There's no telling what the combined power of our sisters everywhere could achieve if they didn't have to bear with some of the issues they had to deal with on the home front. This is a day I long to see, and this is the way I believe we are best able to make it happen!

THE RESPONSIBILITY OF OUR YOUTH

Listen, we know it's been a long time since Martin Luther King marched for our civil rights and our communities were desegregated. It's been an even longer time since the emancipation proclamation was signed, freeing our ancestors from slavery. So yes things have changed, and the conditions for our people have improved a great deal since then there is no question about that. Nevertheless, there are two concepts we need our young people to embrace and pass on through their own descendants.

First, it's important for us to remember that just because things are culturally better for us (at the moment) doesn't mean it's over and our work is done. Far too often I've heard today's youth respond in a lackadaisical, nonchalant manner when questioned about racism and the black plight. It's as if it were some wild beast that went extinct a hundred years ago and can no longer threaten us.

This attitude is careless, usually spoken by those who have a considerable amount of white friends and possibly even related to them by blood, marriage, or adoption. I also maintain good strong bonds with whites (and other races) that I highly treasure and value even more so than certain blacks I know. So, trust me when I say I understand.

However, having these relationships should not interfere with our sense of cultural awareness or activism when dealing with prejudice and injustice against our people. They furthermore should not be used as justifiable reasons to ignore racism when it occurs. Despite the bonds we all may hold outside of the race, we must find ways to stick together and support each other.

I think it's important to note, there have "always" been good whites in our society. There were good whites who opposed slavery from the beginning. There were good whites who assisted us in escaping from slavery as well. There were good whites who marched with Dr. King to help repeal Jim Crow laws in the south, and the nation still has plenty of good whites who voted for and supported the election of our first Black President Barack Obama.

Therefore, it would be hypocritical and contradictory to attempt to generalize the entire Caucasian race (or any other race for that matter) as all being of one mind or opinion. So, the fact that many of us enjoy respectable relationships with them should not come as a surprise to anyone. It should also be pointed out, that even with the existence of these noble individuals in many cases our situation has remained the same.

This is because the problem is not theirs to solve in the first place. Let's just be sure we don't get confused and misinterpret a few good relationships outside of the culture as a notion of pre-achieved equality for blacks everywhere. We could look at it this way, it's not uncommon for a nation to have allies as it is essential for growth and prosperity. Yet only a fool would favor his or her ties with a **foreign power** over their own homeland and people.

Secondly, I believe it's important to acknowledge that racism & prejudice are an unfortunate part of human nature that will never disappear. It cannot be eliminated from society any more than crime, poverty, or depression. However, some continue to believe it can be permanently defeated. I believe this is probably to provide hope to those who dare to dream.

I find it more realistic to focus on "reducing" the amount of racism and knowing how to properly respond to it when it does flare up in society. Today it has become much more subtle, but it is still there, hiding, and lurking beneath the surface. There's no need to enslave people physically when it can be done economically. They no longer need to lynch us like the Klan when we can be gunned down in the streets by the police. Politically, legally, and economically, the truth is out there if we simply pay attention.

As our children, we only ask that you please take the time to understand our plight. This will make you more prepared should you

The Black Man's Answer

have to endure it and secure the positions needed for our future generations to succeed. If we as parents make a valid attempt to instill these values into you, embrace it, as it will serve as a good foundation to build upon. Your main discipline will be to heed what your elders are teaching and expand upon it in new ways that fit your generation.

If there are no worthy elders around worth listening to, then seek out those who are. Wisdom does not simply fall in your lap. Always take the time to develop yourselves and inspire each other. We do not have a future without our young princes and princesses to rule it for us.

The Answer:

Let's not only guide and educate but include our youth in our activism. Remember, actions speak louder than words. This is why it's important for them to not only respect the ideals passed on, but to also have the discipline to continue the efforts in whatever ways they see fit.

This way it ceases to be our struggle and becomes theirs as the torch is successfully passed from one generation to the next. Let's face it, times change and many of the old ways have already ran their course. It takes new fresh minds to find brand new ways of thinking that will make things happen. This is a task that can only be completed by our up and coming youth.

THE RESPONSIBILITY OF OUR BUSINESSES

There are many who would argue we have gained a certain amount of progress as far as our businesses are concerned. However, it seems most progress remains individualistic. It would be nice if those of us with the means to do more would get together and establish something like a franchise of black owned grocery stores for instance. This way we could tell our folks and local organizations to do business with them and help each other out so jobs could be created for us all.

If successful the network could even expand internationally. Similar to a Wal-Mart, or McDonalds, especially to other black nations in need of commerce. This would allow the original investors to acquire great wealth while stimulating job growth at home and abroad. Is this really an impossible dream? If the answer is no, then why aren't we doing it?

I've found most of our neighborhoods contain local businesses such as barber shops, beauty salons, rib shacks, child daycares, Jamaican or soul food restaurants, etc. Unfortunately, it's been rare that I've witnessed any actual networking between them. They usually do things such as hosting small social events like festivals at the local park, or community functions like catering or food vending at a concert or Gospel music show.

Our small business owners need to understand they are the pillars of our communities and can wield quite a bit of power and influence if properly united. Once combined we could achieve anything from employing those within our community to establishing our own Credit Unions. The sky really is the limit.

It's only possible though if our business owners have the vision to see beyond their own self interest and the discipline to seek out others to pursuit it. The interesting thing is, to whoever is successful at accomplishing this economic unity, the potential to increase their wealth will usually exceed whatever amount they all earn individually.

This connection has to be made at some point in order to progress further than where we currently are, otherwise we remain separate and weak. This will only leave us competing with each other for customers and clientele while dealing with our issues individually. If we continue to conduct business in this manner we become vulnerable for other cultures to come in, set up shop, and build their fortune off our people.

Once that happens we are left with no choice but to pay their prices and hope they have positions left to hire us to work for them in their establishments. I for one don't see how we can ever progress if the majority of us are always seeking employment from businesses founded by outside entities.

The Answer:

When it comes to business there is no standing still. There are only those going up and others coming down. If you're standing still it's just a matter of time until you start going down. In my experience, most small businesses in our communities are standing still. They aren't really looking to expand location wise nor establish an online presence.

Then often when the original owner who had the vision dies, the business goes with them or is sold to someone else who doesn't operate the same way. This loses the magic that made the business work to begin with. To prevent this from happening we must devote time to network and communicate with those entities around us.

This will increase our abilities to make sure we reap at least a percentage of the benefits. In time progress will show, and there will be plenty of respect, prestige, and notoriety for those who were able to hold it together and make it happen for the rest of us.

THE RESPONSIBILITY OF OUR ORGANIZATIONS

I'm sure we have all heard of organizations such as the NAACP, the Black Caucus, and others as well, but how many of us common black citizens can speak on what they actually do on a day to day basis? I'm not saying they aren't important or needed, but if the very community you claim to represent and serve is unaware of who you are and what service you provide, doesn't that kind of defeat the point? I mean as a black man in America when do I get to call this organization that claims to be for the advancement of our race? Also, how do I tell my children to support or become part of this organization when I'm not even sure if they are beneficial for our communities?

For instance, the last time I checked the Southside of Chicago has been a disaster zone for blacks in America for as long as I can remember. Even the popular TV show "Good Times" depicted the situation of a black family who lived in Chicago and couldn't seem to catch a break in the low income area they lived in. Finally the character of the father of this family ended up being shot by the same violence that plagues this city in reality to this day. Even though the characters in this show were made up, their situation was very real.

There are countless numbers of us going through these conditions or worse, not only in Chicago but in multiple other cities across the nation as well. I simply want to know what these current "black organizations" have done and are doing to make it better for us? To most of us at ground level, it seems like very little and I consider that to be a problem. It sometimes appears that strife between different races is the only thing that concerns them. I personally believe anything that does not fulfill its intended purpose needs to be disposed of as it has either become tainted by outside entities or obsolete altogether.

In any case, I feel new organizations should be built that truly serve the "**current**" needs of our people. We need positive organizations with strong agendas on actively and openly addressing our daily basic issues whatever they may be. We need groups headed by individuals who are prepared to address these issues at the city, state, and federal level. Those are the types of organizations I'm looking to support and endorse.

The Black Man's Answer

In short, we need a little more than some group that gives scholarships and awards out once in a while to a select few while charging membership fees to anyone who wants to be affiliated. Although it's nice to know that some wealthy philanthropists can donate to the United Negro College Fund or other black charities for an easy tax write off. However, we need more in place to build a secure foundation for our people.

It's time we produce a new system of cultural representatives who care about the issues that are currently rising in our communities. Some of the current groups in place have become all prestige and very little action. In some cases, they serve as a haven for an "upper class" black society who feels they are somehow removed from the rest of us.

Let's be honest, a group like the NAACP has not been respected in the hood since the civil rights era. Not because they don't do anything, but I feel their agenda has gotten reduced to "handpicking" situations that are worthy of their attention. This usually means an issue has to get national news coverage in order to get a response from them. Well if that's the case, then I may as well call my senator or write my congressman, I mean what's the difference?

Sure, these groups list all the issues affecting our communities. They make great arguments about all the work they've done for the benefit of our people as well. They compile data, research, statistics, and take photo opportunities whenever convenient to maintain a decent image and good publicity. However, the truth lies in the hearts and minds of the African American citizens of this country.

I would wager that if blacks from multiple cities throughout America were surveyed and asked what benefits these groups provided for us, the percentages of those who could provide valid examples would be very low. I also bet the majority of good things mentioned would come from accomplishments they had back during the civil rights era.

This is a problem because it is a new day. Many of the everyday issues that make black life hard aren't worthy of news coverage, but they are problems that need to be dealt with nonetheless. What makes it worse is very few of us know how to get things moving that will cause the change we need. So, I for one think it's time to get some people together who have the discipline to put the needs of their people before their wallet and ego.

The Answer:

As I said before, if it's not working let's get rid of it and move on. We just need to make sure whatever organization we form has the discipline to keep the needs of its people at the forefront. Otherwise, it will eventually become as useless as the system it was meant to replace.

THE RESPONSIBILITY OF OUR CHURCHES

Like many southern blacks I grew up in the church. We all hooted and hollered, shouted & praised the Lord as well as we could. I'm sure many of you can relate to a similar experience. However, if you are like me you probably noticed as time passed over the years we began to realize things that caused many of us to question the integrity of the church, and our faith. In some cases we may have stopped going to church altogether.

Certain issues may have been prevalent in the church such as adultery, pride, jealousy, selfishness, judgmental views, and poor money management to name a few. If the sins of humanity are allowed to invade and effectively corrupt the church, then the people who flocked there as a refuge from those things slowly begin to lose trust in the entire system.

What happened to the church of yester-year when the pastor was the pillar of the community and had a finger on the pulse of all the important issues that affected us? They actively encouraged voting, and some even endorsed candidates they knew would benefit our community. It was not uncommon for many churches to do business and network within the local economy.

Some church leaders even had enough pull with the local Judge and Sherriff downtown to get our youth a little leniency when arrested on juvenile offenses. They would even show up in court to testify on their behalf. We need the kind of churches that produced leaders like Dr. King, Reverend Jessie Jackson, and Reverend Al Sharpton. The kind of church the Ku Klux Klan would attempt to burn down out of fear of what we were planning on the inside. What happened to that strength and magic the black church used to wield within our communities?

These days there's not much need to burn down our churches since few of them push to strengthen, develop, or protect the communities around them. Most Christians are content to simply sit nice and quietly amongst themselves only to quote scriptures, sing hymns, and participate in ceremonies over and over again from the same book that they've must have read over a hundred times.

Now with that being said, there are churches out there who are very much making a difference in their communities and to them I say thank you and keep it up. To the others, and the Christians who attend them, I would hope they continued to improve on their purpose in our communities.

Ask yourselves, when is the last time our church produced a good leader for our community? Or had someone come down to the courthouse to speak on behalf of our youth to keep them from being tried as adults or being made "examples of"? Or at a minimum pass the collection plate around to help someone cover their bills, or raise money for a scholarship?

During election time does your church provide info on who's running for office and why it would or wouldn't be beneficial for you to endorse them? How about the economy, can your pastor get you or your loved one a job if needed? The truth is I've rarely been to a church that could do these things, maybe one or two at best. But you'd better believe the things that were always present were the shouting, praise, and the passing of that collection plate.

It seems in many places today's black church is only a shadow of its former self. Our community must remember that the church and its power, should not be confined to the walls of the building they speak in. Nor by the time limit set on Sunday school service or bible study. The power resonates within the hearts, minds, and spirits of those who worship there. Therefore, as with anything else that great passion and effort is put into, the people need to see some sort of tangible return on their efforts.

If we have people who are relying on government assistance, and the church is asking for a ten percent tithe of that government assistance, then it should come as no surprise when these individuals realize they may as well stay home. This way they can keep that extra ten percent and watch football, or get their hair done on Sundays. If you think about it, any other club or organization that you pay a fee for owes you a clear breakdown of the services you should expect to receive, and this should be no different with the church considering the tithes and offerings it takes in on a regular basis.

Also, the church should take Gods people to places where they are needed. If the only place you and your congregation ever goes is to visit other churches, then there's some work to be done. As far as the members are concerned, we Christians who attend the church must have enough sense to "**request**" the services we need in our communities. The preacher may simply not know, he is only one man after all so it can't all be left up to him. Church members must hold the staff accountable and ensure the pastor stays sharp and actively engaged in the issues that matter in the community.

If our ideas are not met with a sincere effort, then that is a good indicator that it may be time to search for a new place of worship. A better church, one where the pastor has truly been called to serve by God. This you will know because the anointing can be seen not only in him but in the congregation that serves him and the work the ministries do within the community.

This is the only way to weed out those false prophets amongst us who abuse the divine position of preacher for prestige, improper relations, and financial gain. It will require great discipline, and due diligence in our research of churches in order to make this happen.

The Answer:

It may not stand true for all but for many the church has some work to do. Not just in the ways of religious doctrine, but in the ways of social order. Moral decay has risen and is extremely high in our American society. In order to reduce the negative energy and help replace honor in our communities, our place of worship must strengthen to provide guidance and sanctuary from the ills of society.

It will take discipline from our religious leaders to ensure the church can provide this and serve as the beacon of salvation it should be. Instead of just another system in place meant to control or exploit us.

Chapter 13
Selflessness

THE END RESULT

The gift of selflessness is something frequently wished for and rarely received or practiced. Not just among our people but by everyone in humanity. As kids we often looked for things to make us feel happy and taken care of. At Christmas we rushed to see what gifts were under the tree, but rarely were we concerned about whether gifts were under the trees in the homes of others in our neighborhoods. The same happens on other occasions such as Halloween, or Birthdays for instance. I didn't know very many kids who were naturally willing to give up or share the candy earned from a hard night of trick-or-treating. Although if they did the best candy was usually kept for themselves.

Likewise, when it came to Birthdays, many of us wanted a grand celebration for the occasion to invite everyone we knew to make the event successful and memorable "**for us**". If any of us felt we didn't get the treatment we deserved on our special day, we began to resent those who we felt were responsible for neglecting us. In some cases, we even questioned their love for us altogether.

Now for those of us who "did" receive the happy holidays and treatment we wanted, how likely was it that we as kids showed our appreciation by offering to clean up after the party? Or remembering everyone who attended so we could return the favor? To be honest not many kids do, and most of the ones who do were usually guilt tripped into it by their parents.

I can speak for myself when I say I very rarely thought of doing anything for anyone other than myself. I rarely even remember saying "thank you" when something was done nice for me. Not that I was mean or anything, it's just the kind of kid I was. The reason I point this out is because a lot of us don't understand that being "selfish" is; **(1)** something we all are born with, capable of, and do regularly, and **(2)** that it takes work and practice to instill the good habits and values needed to overcome it.

Unfortunately, "something for nothing" is what many people end up seeking when approaching others for help and assistance in this world. Often looking to appeal to one's kind heart, good nature, or in some cases even their sense of religious duty. We all love morals but at the end of the day we can't use them only when it's convenient. Many of us seek attention from those we seldom give any attention to in return. We seek protection from those we rarely protect back. We also demand understanding from those we have yet to understand ourselves.

We must get to a point where we as a people become known for thinking of our fellow man. I know it's a long way away, but I do believe it is possible. One day when we are able to overcome the issues that plague us as a whole can we become a dependable community for other cultures as well. No longer would our neighborhoods be synonymous with words like ghetto, poverty, crime, and ignorance.

Everyone would be striving to keep themselves and our neighbor's well being in the forefront of our thoughts and actions. Thus, laying the foundation down for a great nation and a time of beautiful prosperity for our people. Networking would increase as neighboring cultures develop a newfound sense of respect and trust for us once it becomes clear that resources can flow "**OUT**" of our community for the aid of others, instead of always needing to flow "**IN**" to help ourselves.

Epilogue

REGARDING THOSE WHO ARE INDIFFERENT

There are many of us out there who have simply gotten in too deep to turn back. These individuals either like how things are now or may not believe further change is possible. In some cases they may share our skin tone but not identify with the majority of us within the race. They have determined our struggle is not something they should concern themselves with. They tend to believe we should be grateful for where we are now, and that blacks of today really have nothing to complain about since no one alive today has ever been enslaved.

They are typically known for avoiding any issues involving race, slavery, or anything that may prevent them from blending in with mainstream America. In some cases, they honestly may not have experienced direct hate or discrimination from anyone at all. This means they don't have the history needed to make a decent argument about inequalities or civil rights. In this day and age this is becoming a reality for more and more of us, and we simply don't know how to handle it.

It's ok because everyone's entitled to their own beliefs, views, and opinions. I only ask that should you come across others who do believe and are doing their best to make a difference in this world, to please not discourage them. Some of the hardest critics I have had to face have been other blacks who did not see a reason or purpose for me to continue going on about the inequities our people have had to face.

I can honestly say this was the biggest obstacle of all for me in completing this book because if my own people didn't support what

I was doing then all my ideals were virtually dead before they got off the ground. The last thing I wanted to do was get torn to shreds by the "**educated**" black community concerning our struggles. Especially since I was just an average brother trying to spark a little awareness into my people. Needless to say the fear and self doubt was almost enough to make me quit.

So, if you should know someone who shows some promise of uniqueness amongst our people, then nurture it. There's no telling what they could turn out to be in life. These individuals are hard to come by and we need them in order to progress. Therefore let's do what we can to look out for them because, they could end up meaning a lot for the future of our people.

Q & A

Below is a list of the most frequently asked questions I have encountered when discussing my views of the Black plight with others in our society.

Question: Blacks today have never experienced slavery or segregation, so at this point what exactly are African Americans fighting for and why?

Answer: As African Americans we still have much work to do in terms of rebuilding our culture, increasing our wealth, and unifying our political and economic resources. We need this to achieve the lives we desire. Today's challenge resides amongst ourselves more so than against others.

Question: In your book you referenced some issues dealing with blacks marrying outside of their culture, so does this mean you don't believe in interracial dating?

Answer: I believe people should be free to love whomever they choose. To try and control such a thing would be a waste of time. I only ask that you properly honor and cherish the person who you've chosen to reproduce with, while maintaining the culture and identity of who you are as a person. This is needed for the happiness and internal peace within yourself, your spouse, and any future children you may have.

Question: What are your feelings concerning Pan-Africanism?

Answer: I think Pan-Africanism is a good idea for some who have that particular fire burning in their heart. However, I don't see it as a practical remedy for the majority of our people. In many cases the vast nations of Africa have their own issues, situations I fear that anyone trying to relocate may find just as problematic if not more so than the ones they left behind here in America.

Question: Do you believe blacks should continue to practice a religion that was forced upon us by our oppressors?
Answer: I am a man of God. So, when it comes to religion, I'd advise people to go wherever they feel the presence of God exists.

Question: So when will it be "over" so to speak? How will blacks know when they have gotten to a point where they can rest and not worry about racism and equality?
Answer: Well that's just it, there is no end to it. It is simply part of the basic fight for our survival. There is no life form that does not have to fight in order to continue its existence in this world, and so it stands to be the same for the black man. We just need to ensure we don't forget this and keep working vigilantly to improve our future in this world.

Question: So let's assume everyone hears your concerns from this book and agrees to come together for a common cause, what would be the next step?
Answer: The next step would be to designate the proper people in specialized fields (who are a lot more qualified than myself) to lay the blueprints down for the things our people need in various areas of our communities. Then from that point on we can all share in the shaping of our culture for the future, which is the way it should be.

Question: Do you really feel partnering with the Hispanic community would be a beneficial move for African Americans?
Answer: Absolutely! They are fighting many of the same battles we are and I believe we could benefit from each other's strength and resources. Also, in my mind Latinos aren't too far from being Native

Americans anyway. Their ancestors just occupied a more southern part of the Americas. It would be interesting to do some DNA testing to see if the ones many are calling "illegal immigrants" aren't in fact closer to being the original citizens of this nation.

Question: What about those blacks who disagree with your ideals, what is your response to them?
Answer: Well, everyone is entitled to their own opinion and I respect that. Truthfully though they don't have to agree with me. They could follow their own ideals in their own ways and as long as it brought positive effects to themselves or our culture, I would be in full support of it!

Question: Would there be a place for whites and other "non-blacks" to participate in the events if so desired?
Answer: Of course! All are welcome who have a genuine and sincere desire to contribute to our cause!

Question: According to your book it would seem you do not like the idea of blacks receiving reparations for slavery, is this true?
Answer: I am not opposed to our culture being awarded reparations for slavery. I am however opposed to us sitting around complaining about the fact that no one is giving us something. I think we've seen enough "benign neglect" from our government at this point to know we will never receive that 40 acres or the mule.

Question: Do you believe the black leaders of the civil rights era had the right idea with integration, or do you believe more harm than good was done to the black community in the long run?
Answer: I have nothing but love, admiration, and respect for all who fought for change back in that era. They were definitely the warriors needed to stand up for us at that time. However, they couldn't have solved "**ALL**" of the problems for our people by themselves, nor should they have been expected to. Now as the new generation we

simply have to continue the same fight to make sure we don't lose the ground they gained for us. It's a new battle, with a new set of rules that require a different breed of warriors. Any failures or shortcomings we endure today, is officially our responsibility. We can never blame it on those that came before us.

Bibliography

1. Bivens, Josh/Gould, Elise/Mishel, Lawrence/Shierholz, Heidi. "African American Fact Sheet", *The State of Working America, 12th Edition,* www.stateofworkingamerica.org. The economic policy institute www.epi.org, September 4th 2012.

2. Deshay, Akiim. "Marriage in Black America", *Black Demographics,* www.blackdemographics.com, January 1st 2014.

3. National Kids Count Data Center, "Children in single parent families by race", *National Kids Count Data Center,* www.datacenter.kidscount.org. The Annie E. Casey Foundation, www.aecf.org, January 1st 2017.

4. Zook, Kristal. "Blacks own just ten television stations, here's why", *The Washington Post,* www.washingtonpost.com, August 17th 2015.

5. Mouzon, Dawne. "Why Has Marriage Declined among Black Americans?" *Scholars Strategy Network,* www.scholarsstrategynetwork.org, October 1st 2013.

f

6. Lee, Jeanne. "Why America Needs Black Owned Banks", *USA Today*, www.usatoday.com, February 16th 2017.

7. United States Census Bureau. "Gap between Higher and Lower Wealth households widens", *United States Census Bureau,* www.census.gov, August 21st 2014.

8. Deshay, Akiim. "Occupations of African Americans", *Black Demographics,* www.blackdemographics.com, United States Census Bureau, www.census.gov, June 1st 2012.

9. Krogstad, Jens/Lopez, Mark. "Black voter turnout fell in 2016, even as a record number of Americans cast ballots", *Pew Research Center,* www.pewresearch.org, May 12th 2017.

10. United States Census Bureau. "Statistics for All U.S. Firms by Industry, Gender, Ethnicity, and Race for the U.S., States, Metro Areas, Counties, and Places: 2012 Survey of Business Owners", *United States Census Bureau,* www.census.gov, December 15th 2015.

11. Puglise, Nicole. "Black Americans incarcerated five times more than white people – report", *The Guardian,* www.theguardian.com, June 18th 2016.

12. The Journal of Blacks in Higher Education. "More Than 4.5 Million African Americans Now Hold a Four-Year College Degree", *The Journal of Blacks in Higher Education.* www.jbhe.com, June 1st 2010.

13. American Heart Association. "African-Americans and Heart Disease, Stroke", *American Heart Association,* www.heart.org, July 1st 2015.

14. Jones-Webb, Rhonda Dr. P.H. "Drinking Patterns and Problems among African Americans: Recent Findings", *National Institute on Alcohol Abuse and Alcoholism,* www.niaaa.nih.gov, August 1st 1998.

15. Health and Human Services Office of Minority Health, "Mental Health and African Americans", *Health and Human Services Office of Minority Health,* minorityhealth.hhs.gov, September 15th 2017.